CREATING BEDS
and BORDERS

fine
Gardening Design Guides

CREATING BEDS
and BORDERS

Creative Ideas *from* America's Best Gardeners

The Taunton Press

Special thanks to the editors, art directors, copy editors, and other staff members of Fine Gardening *who contributed to the development of the articles in this book.*

Front cover photographers: Gary Irving (large), Lee Anne White, © The Taunton Press, Inc. (inset)
Back cover photographers: Lee Anne White, © The Taunton Press, Inc. (large);
Bard Wrigley (Erica Glasener photo); all other photos courtesy *Fine Gardening*
magazine, © The Taunton Press, Inc.
Publisher: Jim Childs
Acquisitions Editor: Lee Anne White
Editorial Assistant: Meredith DeSousa
Technical Editor: Todd Meier
Copy Editor: Candace Levy
Indexer: Linda Stannard
Art Director: Paula Schlosser
Design Manager: Rosalind Wanke
Cover and Interior Designer: Lori Wendin
Layout Artists: Susan Fazekas, Jennifer Wyzykowski

Taunton
BOOKS & VIDEOS
for fellow enthusiasts

Printed in the United States of America
10 9 8 7 6 5 4 3 2 1

The Taunton Press, Inc., 63 South Main Street, PO Box 5506,
Newtown, CT 06470-5506
e-mail: tp@taunton.com

Distributed by Publishers Group West

Library of Congress Cataloging-in-Publication Data
Creating beds and borders : creative ideas from America's best gardeners.
p. cm.—(Fine gardening design guides)
ISBN 1-56158-473-8
1. Beds (Gardens). 2. Garden borders. 3. Plants, Ornamental.
4. Beds (Gardens—United States). 5. Garden borders—United States.
6. Plants, Ornamental—United States. I. Fine gardening. II. Series.
SB423.7.B49   2001
635.9'63—dc21   00-059936

"Creating a border means juggling several balls in the air simultaneously. Plant height, spread, color, foliage, and the season of bloom must all be orchestrated to form a symphony of ongoing color combinations."

—Barbara Blossom Ashmun
The Garden Design Primer

Contents

Introduction

Beds and borders are often the highlight of a garden—the place where we grow our most cherished plants and where we strive to create show-stopping color in one season or less conspicuous, yet continuous bloom from spring through fall. They are, in most cases, the most decorative plantings in the garden.

When you design a bed or border, you have to consider its location, design, soil preparation, and plantings. Will your border be placed in a sunny spot against a white picket fence or in the shade on the north side of your house? Or do you prefer a series of freestanding beds in your lawn? Will their shape be formal or informal, geometric or curving? Do you need to remove sod and amend your soil? What shall you plant, and in what combination for best effect?

In *Creating Beds & Borders*, some of America's best gardeners will walk you through those decisions. For years, they've been sharing their insights in *Fine Gardening* magazine. Now, you have their work in a single book that you can take with you out in the yard for inspiration and ideas. They'll teach you how to dig a new bed without breaking your back, how to best use a variety of plants in a border, and how to maintain your borders both through the summer and over the years. You'll also discover a gallery of unique beds and borders filled with innovative ideas and creative solutions for challenging situations.

DESIGN
STRATEGIES

1

BORDERS ARE PLANTING BEDS with a background. They are placed in front of walls, fences, and hedges. And they are typically viewed only from one side. Beds are freestanding islands placed in a lawn or perhaps in a courtyard setting. Either can be formal or informal. Quite often, they are formal in design (with a series of geometric beds), but informal in their approach to planting.

Where should you place your border? How big should an island bed be? How do you go about organizing the plants so that they can all be seen or hiding the ugly legs of taller perennials? In this section, we'll explore the basics of designing a bed or border—taking a look at siting, size, and structure.

BARBARA BLOSSOM ASHMUN

is a garden designer, the author of several books, including *Garden Retreats* and *The Garden Design Primer*, and a contributing editor for *Fine Gardening*.

Bed & Border

Basics

Linked by lawn, curving beds and borders organize the author's backyard into separate planting areas. A mass of purple *Veronica spicata* enlivens the foreground bed. (Photo taken at A on site plan, p. 11.)

ONE OF THE MOST versatile ways to design a garden that is rich in flowering plants and still appears unified is to divide the property into beds and borders. I'm mad about flowers, and so are the clients of my garden-design business, but we want our gardens to look like more than collections of plants. Beds and borders help us accomplish our goal.

What are beds and borders? Island beds are free-standing planting areas that you can walk around and view from all sides. They may be round, oval, rectangular, square or irregular in shape and are usually surrounded by lawn. Borders are generally made against a backdrop, such as a hedge, fence, wall, building or property line, and are usually viewed from only one side. Borders can have a straight or a curving edge—it usually follows the line of the backdrop.

I use beds and borders in my garden designs because they're versatile. They can help you organize your garden

Sedum 'Autumn Joy' nestles beneath peach-flowered daylilies on the streetside of the author's front border. Easy-to-grow perennials, daylilies readily establish themselves in a new border or bed.

Finally, beds and borders allow you to work on your garden one piece at a time.

I want time to get to know a garden, understand the light, the wind, the existing trees and the shape of the land. I also need a chance to experiment, learn, improve the soil, dream, imagine and create. The day-dreaming kind of trance I put myself in to create a garden does not happen under pressure. You can develop new areas of your property in beds and borders as your time, energy and budget allow. You can create a full look and a sense of satisfaction even if other parts of the property are not complete. And you can easily re-do one bed or border without disrupting the rest of the garden.

SOLVING COMMON PROBLEMS

My property started with common problems—lack of privacy and unwelcome views. I bought it for its mainly sunny exposure, relatively flat terrain and ample gardening space. Although the property is 100 ft. wide and 300 ft. deep, the house sits only 40 ft. from the road. For the front yard, I wanted privacy and a nice view to enjoy from the kitchen and living room windows, as well as streetside plantings that would attract clients. In the backyard, I wanted to screen out the neighbors' yards on the south and west. I also hoped to block the view of wild areas that I wasn't ready to tackle. Beds and borders proved to be ideal building blocks for my garden. They made it easy for me to develop it slowly, but with purpose.

A BORDER THAT LOOKS TWO WAYS

The border I created along the street at the edge of my front lawn provides privacy and beauty. It's home to a mixed planting of trees,

into distinct areas, each with a specific purpose. For example, a border of tall, screening plants will give privacy from the neighbors, while crescent-shaped beds near a patio or swimming pool can create a feeling of enclosure and intimacy. Planting in beds and borders is also a convenient way to group together plants best-suited for problem sites, such as areas with poorly drained soil or a windy exposure. Because they're self-contained, beds and borders offer flexibility in design. They can be made in different shapes and sizes and still mix well together in one garden.

A backbone of tall shrubs helps create privacy in the front yard.

Upright and mounding perennials fill the middle of the border.

Low-growing and ground-hugging plants edge the border, following the contour of lawn. (Photo taken at B on site plan, p. 11.)

Plantings of perennials on either side of the shrubs offer colorful views from both the house and street.

shrubs, perennials, annuals and bulbs that can be enjoyed from two sides—from the house and from the street. A backbone of small trees and shrubs down the center of the border partially screens the road from my view and also blocks the house from the view of passersby. Against this backdrop, I planted drifts of perennials, bulbs and annuals on the house side for my enjoyment and big sweeps of bright perennials along the street for onlookers.

Separating the border into two sides allowed me to work with two different color schemes. Facing the house, I planted mainly flowers in the softer hues I prefer—pale blues, pinks, purples, soft yellows, with a touch of white. Toward the road, I experimented with vibrant

"To create privacy, I planted shrubs and trees, all 8 ft. to 10 ft. tall, in the center of the border."

oranges, reds, yellows and blues, colors to stop traffic and attract pedestrians and runners.

Although I wanted my side of the border to look interesting year-round, I began by planning the winter view from the kitchen, thinking that winter is when I most need to see cheerful colors. I started with a composition of *Viburnum × bodnantense* 'Dawn', a shrub whose small, clove-scented, pink flowers bloom in winter, and masses of lenten roses (*Helleborus orientalis*), a low perennial whose shapely evergreen leaves are covered with delicate pink and cream-colored flowers in February and March.

To create privacy, I planted shrubs and trees, all 8 ft. to 10 ft. tall, in the center of the border. I chose a white-flowered saucer magnolia (*Magnolia × soulangeana* 'Lennei Alba') for spring color, a pink rose (*Rosa glauca*) for early summer color and red fall fruits and a sassafras tree (*Sassafras albidum*) for its orange fall color. They don't completely screen out the road, but they do give me a feeling of separation and enclosure. And they look much more interesting than an evergreen hedge.

Lower shrubs and tall perennials enrich the picture. Facing the house, I planted spring-flowering, fragrant shrubs: pink-flowered daphnes (*Daphne × burkwoodii* 'Somerset' and 'Carol Mackie') and a Meyer lilac (*Syringa meyeri*). I added clumps of Japanese and Siberian iris (*I. ensata* and *I. sibirica*). Closer to

Moisture-loving plants are grouped together in this low-lying island bed

The sword-like foliage of yellow flag iris serves as a striking accent.

Ceramic fish, made by sculptor Katy McFadden, frolic among the iris foliage.

The gently curved edge of the bed lends a graceful, flowing look to the garden.

'Claridge Druce' geraniums edge the border, providing contrast in shape and color to surrounding plants.

the front of the border, I placed pink and white summer phlox (*Phlox paniculata*), valerian (*Valeriana officinalis*), which bears white, fragrant flowers, and, to jazz things up, peonies in shades of pink and dark pink-red. Framing the border are masses of lady's mantle (*Alchemilla mollis*), with its foamy sprays of yellow flowers, blue-flowered hardy geraniums (*Geranium himalayense*) and dusty pink-flowered *Sedum* 'Autumn Joy'.

In late spring, the streetside of the border bursts forth with the intense colors of red-orange Oriental poppies (*Papaver orientale*), purple Siberian irises and fragrant, yellow-flowered lemon daylilies (*Hemerocallis bilioasphodelus)*. For summer color, I massed yellow and salmon-pink daylilies (*H.* spp.), yellow threadleaf coreopsis (*Coreopsis verticillata*) and blue Frikart's aster (*Aster* × *frikartii*). For fall, I planted drifts of dwarf asters in shades of blue and purple, orange montbretia (*Crocosmia* × *crocosmiiflora*) and red California fuchsia (*Zauschneria californica*), a low-growing sprawler. This side of the border is a wonderful four-season feature and a real people-stopper. I am so happy when I discover that the beauty I've helped to create is being enjoyed by so many others.

A BED FOR A WET SITE

My "damp-garden" bed deals with two problems: an eyesore and wet, boggy ground. The eyesore, a 7-ft.-diameter cistern that the previous owner had filled with debris and topped with soil, temporarily fills with water during heavy winter rains, giving it the appearance of a small pond. My property also drains down to this area, so all the ground in front of the cistern is quite damp as well. Turning a liability into an asset, I made the cistern a focal point for a damp garden. Within the cistern I planted irises that thrive in standing water—yellow

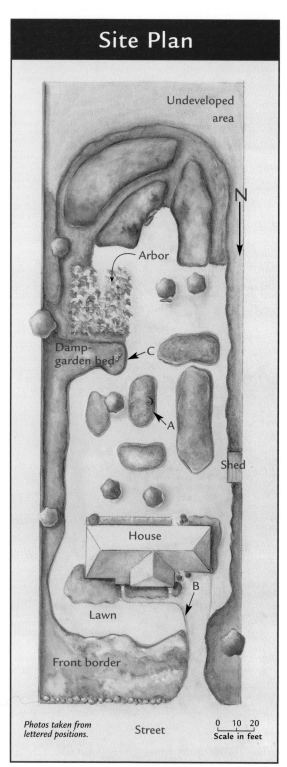

Site Plan

Undeveloped area

Arbor

Damp-garden bed

C

A

Shed

House

B

Lawn

Front border

Photos taken from lettered positions.

Street

0 10 20
Scale in feet

flag iris (*Iris pseudacorus*) and the blue form of *I. virginica*. Next to the cistern, I planted blue Siberian iris and white spuria iris (*I. spuria*) along with astilbes (*Astilbe* × *arendsii*) in shades of pink, red and creamy white. These plants love the damp soil and flourish in this

Sunlight dances off the flowers of a hardy geranium (*Geranium endressii*).

need arose. For example, my first bed covered some bare ground left in the wake of the previous owner's trailer home; the next bed united several roses that were sprinkled around the lawn. A fall delivery of irises created an emergency need for a third bed, which I hastily made by topping the lawn with 18 in. of compost and planting directly into it. (Plants in this raised bed, with its excellent drainage, have grown the most vigorously of all.)

Despite the wide assortment of plants in the individual beds, the garden holds together visually. My upper backyard, for example, is tied together by a series of round beds. Making more than one bed of a similar shape helps create a feeling of unity, as does a carpet of grass winding between them. The green grass also gives the eyes relief from flower color.

STALWART PLANTS FOR NEW BEDS AND BORDERS

I use stalwart plants, tried and true perennials that survive difficult situations without any pampering, to break new ground. I recommend you start with these plants when you make a new bed or border. They establish well, multiply quickly and are easy to move.

For heavy clay soil that stays wet in winter and spring, I rely on Siberian iris, daylilies and hardy geraniums. Siberian irises grow in strong clumps with vertical, blade-like green leaves topped by purple, blue, magenta-pink or white flowers. Plants grow from 2 ft. to 5 ft. tall and expand to 3 ft. across by their third year in the garden. Some of my favorites are deep purple 'Caesar's Brother', vibrant pink-red 'Eric the Red' and burgundy 'Chilled Wine'. The irises are striking when they bloom in early summer

site, which is shady in the morning and quite sunny in the afternoon. In front of the Siberian iris, I grow daylilies in shades of creamy yellow and salmon-pink, and I edge the bed with lady's-mantle and hardy geraniums.

My beds and borders are small worlds within the larger garden. I developed each as the and restful afterwards, when their foliage serves as a good backdrop for later-blooming flowers. These deep-rooted plants tolerate sun or part shade and standing water.

Daylilies are also clump-forming perennials; they have grassy, outwardly arching leaves, and flowers in shades of yellow, orange, peach, pink, red, lavender or white. It's hard to choose from the abundant offerings. The blooms are big, but last only one day. The spent flowers look like rumpled socks or crumpled crepe paper, so it's important to pick them off frequently or plant the daylilies where they will be viewed only from a distance. In my front border, these plants have come through six winters of standing water and full sun with flying colors. They have also survived elsewhere in my garden in partial shade and in dry places.

Hardy geraniums range from small ground covers to large border specimens. They'll grow in sun or partial shade, in dry or wet soil. And they are beautiful, besides.

The ones I count on for ground-breaking are *G. pratense, G. himalayense, G. ibericum* and *G. endressii*. Of these, *G. pratense* is the weediest, spreading from roots and self-seeding, but it's a lot prettier than the dandelions I'd have in its place. It stands 3 ft. tall and flowers its head off in June, at the same time as the peonies and old roses. It bears an abundance of small, blue-violet flowers among deeply divided leaves. *G. ibericum*, which grows about 1½ ft. tall, has darker blue-violet flowers and works well as a ground cover. My *G. himalayense*, with its lovely blue-violet flowers, grows at the edge of the mixed border near a drift of lady's mantle. The flowers are similar in color to those of *G. ibericum*, but the leaves are more daintily divided. *G. endressii* has bright pink flowers that are almost too intense, and it blooms from summer through autumn. From tiny divisions I took in spring, it spread into a substantial ground cover the first season and flowered all summer. I wish I had thought to plant *G. xoxonianum* 'A.T. Johnson' instead, a cultivar with lighter, creamier pink flowers, but oh well....

For dry shade, two of my favorite perennials are Mrs. Robb's spurge (*Euphorbia amygdaloides* var. *robbiae*) and epimediums (*Epimedium* spp.). The dark green, glossy, evergreen leaves of the spurge form rosettes at ground level. In the spring, flowering stems bearing bright yellow flowers shoot up about 2 ft. tall. The plants spread quickly by underground runners, but you can easily keep them in check by digging out the extras. Be careful to wear gloves when you touch spurge because the milky juice inside the stems can irritate your skin and eyes.

There are many epimedium species. Most are evergreen, and all are tolerant of dry situations. Delightful plants for the shade, they bear medium-green, heart-shaped leaves and early spring flowers in shades of yellow, white or pink, depending on the species. My favorite (so far) is *E. × rubrum,* a pink-flowered species. Blooming about the same time as early daffodils, it makes a lovely ground cover beneath flowering crabapples, plums or cherries.

"*My beds and borders are small worlds within the larger garden.*"

NICK SEMINCHUK

has been an avid gardener for more than 15 years. His garden has been featured on HGTV's *The Gardener's Journal* and on several garden tours.

Order *in the* Border

Use shrubs for structure, masses of perennials for color, and annuals to complete the picture.

TEN YEARS AGO, my family and I attended a wedding in a backyard. The whole affair—from the ceremony to the reception—was held in a peaceful garden at the home of the bride's parents. It made such an impression on my daughter Melanie, who was 14 at the time, that, when we got home, she announced her desire to be married in our own backyard. My wife, Wendy, and I looked at each other. We wanted our daughter's dream to come true, but there was one rather significant snag—we didn't have a garden. And to make matters worse, we hardly knew a marigold from a magnolia.

We started reading every gardening magazine we could get our hands on and soon realized the need for a plan. A friend, Gord Rendell, who taught horticulture at a local high school, helped us by sketching out a deep, U-shaped

> *"We bought only a few plants at a time. Then, every other spring, I'd divide them to make new plants."*
>
> ◠

perennial border more than 50 yards long and recommending a number of shrubs for it.

Our initial response to his ambitious plan was sheer bewilderment. How would we ever transform his drawing into a backyard reality and have fun in the process? After the shock wore off, we organized a plan of attack. We'd use the classic recipe—shrubs for structure, masses of perennials for dramatic sweeps of color, and flowering annuals to fill the gaps.

USE SHRUBS TO BUILD THE GARDEN'S BACKBONE

Our first priority was to hire someone to dig the beds and amend our heavy, clay soil with topsoil and peat moss. Once that was done, we planted shrubs that would become the bones—the enduring, structural framework—of the garden. The rest of the garden would be arranged around them.

Gord suggested shrubs that would provide interest in all four seasons and attract birds and butterflies. The eventual size of each shrub was another important consideration. By using large shrubs to swallow up space, we wouldn't have to buy so many plants to fill the vast garden we wanted. Gord's selections also introduced varied shapes, foliage colors, and textures to the border, thereby giving it a more dynamic quality. The plan included purple-leaved sand cherries (*Prunus* × *cistena*), whose reddish purple foliage contrasts beautifully

with an almost luminous, mounded form of variegated tatarian dogwood (*Cornus alba* 'Elegantissima'). For flowers, we added a saucer magnolia (*Magnolia* × *soulangiana*), a few forsythia (*Forsythia* × *intermedia*), and a bridalwreath spirea (*Spiraea prunifolia*). Three Russian olive trees (*Elaeagnus angustifolia*), with their small, silvery canopies, anchor the east side of the flower beds, and a few needled evergreens—several junipers (*Juniperus* spp.), an Alberta spruce (*Picea glauca* 'Nana'), and a few yews (*Taxus* spp.)—provide color even in winter.

WITH PERENNIALS, IT'S MASSES THAT APPEAL

Once the shrubs were planted, we started on the next phase—choosing perennials. We needed plants that wouldn't mind getting their feet wet—our garden can be very damp in spring and fall. Most important, we wanted perennials with a long period of bloom. After poring through countless mail-order catalogs, we compiled a list of plants that would suit our USDA Hardiness Zone 6 garden.

I wanted to use perennials in masses to create a sense of continuity. We'd need hundreds of plants to fill our huge border, but economics dictated a modest start. We bought only a few plants at a time. Then, every other spring, I'd divide them to make new plants. For a few favorites, like black-eyed Susans (*Rudbeckia*

Shrubs and small trees anchor the garden, providing structure and multi-season interest.

Masses of perennials offer a sense of continuity, as drifts of color are repeated over the length of the border.

Annuals fill in bare spots and ensure that the fireworks continue throughout the gardening season.

Create a dramatic sense of three dimensions by moving taller plants such as ornamental grasses to the front of the border.

fulgida 'Goldsturm'), I'd also collect seed to start new plants. In time, I'd have the masses I wanted.

We wanted repeating drifts of color—especially yellows, pinks, and whites—along the length of the border. We welcomed spring with yellow trumpet daffodils (*Narcissus* 'King Alfred')—planted in clumps of eight—and lots of tulips, any variety, as long as the flowers were pink or white. Costs prohibited us from filling the entire border with bulbs at the start, so we added them gradually. We still add 50 to 100 new bulbs, mostly tulips, each fall.

In summer, the same palette prevails. The gardens resound with golden black-eyed Susans, which look great with anything. The borders are also filled with white Shasta daisies (*Leucanthemum* × *superbum*), phlox (*Phlox paniculata*), and white coneflowers (*Echinacea purpurea* 'White Swan'). For fresh-looking pinks, I planted purple coneflowers (*E. purpurea* 'Bright Star') and musk mallow (*Malva moschata*), with its upright clumps of hibiscuslike blooms. Many of these plants bloom for up to nine weeks.

In fall, the palette shifts subtly, as the ruddy flower heads of *Sedum* 'Autumn Joy', and the silvery, plumelike flowers of ornamental grasses take center stage. I especially like silver feather grass (*Miscanthus sinensis* 'Silberfeder') and fountain grass (*Pennisetum alopecuroides*). Asters, mostly the lavender-blue flowers of *Aster × frikartii* 'Monch' and the warm pinks of *A. novae-angliae* 'Alma Potschke', also color the fall.

FILL THE GAPS WITH ANNUALS

To ensure that floral fireworks continue from summer to fall, we fill gaps between the shrubs and perennials with annuals that bloom their hearts out. In the early days of the garden, that meant planting 750 or so each spring. I planted wax begonias (*Begonia × semperflorens-cultorum*) and periwinkle (*Catharanthus roseus*) by the hundreds, and lots of dusty miller (*Centaurea cineraria*). To save money, I purchased the plants as plugs, tiny starts that came 350 to a tray. I also planted impatiens (*Impatiens walleriana*), spider flowers (*Cleome hassleriana*), and cosmos (*Cosmos bipinnatus*).

Now that the shrubs and perennials have filled out, we don't spend as much time or money on annuals. The shrubs have grown into substantial clumps, and the many divisions I've made of perennials have filled the border to bursting. I've also edged the front of the border with perennials like lamb's ears (*Stachys byzantina*), coralbells (*Heuchera* spp.) and lady's mantle (*Alchemilla mollis*). Still, we grow a few favorites from seeds we collect and scatter each fall. The spider flowers are especially abundant, which is fine with us because we love their soft colors and fine presence.

FOR AN INFORMAL LOOK, DON'T STAGGER PLANT HEIGHTS

As our garden matured, we learned to break a few of the design rules advocated by many books and magazines. The greatest reward has come from forsaking the idea of staggered planting—using low plants at the front of the border and tall plants at the rear. For our taste, that's too formal. We prefer the dramatic sense of three dimensions created by placing taller plants, like ornamental grasses and 4-ft.- and 5-ft.-high asters, at the front of the border.

Now that the stage is set, I tend it with care, keeping the lawn lush and the border edged and weeded. All we have to do is to sit back, enjoy, and await that very special day when Melanie fulfills her teenage aspiration.

"We fill gaps between the shrubs and perennials with annuals that bloom their hearts out."

BARBARA BLOSSOM ASHMUN

is a garden designer, the author of several books, including *Garden Retreats* and *The Garden Design Primer*, and a contributing editor for *Fine Gardening*.

Design Island Beds to View from Any Angle

Massing multiple island beds gives the impression of a larger overall garden. When seen from ground level, the beds blend together.

MY FIRST ISLAND BEDS were designed out of necessity to cover two gaps in the lawn—a bare circle of dirt where the former owner parked his recreational vehicle, and a rectangular strip that was once the compost pile. But after visiting Bressingham Gardens in England, where nurseryman Alan Bloom created a demonstration garden consisting of island beds, I came home and really went to town. A decade later, 11 island beds float in a sea of lawn.

DESIGN EACH BED INDIVIDUALLY

Islands are freestanding beds, usually surrounded by grass, but occasionally bordered by brick, stone, or even crushed rock. Each is a small, manageable project, like writing a short story instead of a novel. You can create just one island bed in a gardening season for a satisfying sense of accomplishment without killing yourself.

Broad-leaved plants are best for edging around lawn. Hardy geraniums, which contrast with grassy foliage, are among the author's favorite edging plants.

One advantage of going slowly, one island bed at a time, is that you can learn about plants and develop your own style over a period of years. I've never seen the point of designing and planting a whole garden in one fell swoop—this leaves no room for evolution and discovery. Another reason to add new beds each year is just practical—to have homes for the new cultivars that show up in the nurseries every spring. Islands also provide an easy way to group plants that need the same growing conditions.

Because an island bed is its own contained world, each can have its own color scheme, yet several islands can draw on diverse color schemes without looking too busy. With lawn as a buffer, there's no harm in placing warm colors (oranges, reds, and yellows) and cool colors (blues, greens, and violets) in neighboring beds.

"In a large garden with ample lawn, I like to group several island beds near each other for greater impact."

Weeding, deadheading, and mulching in island beds is pleasurable work because plants are accessible from all sides. It's also easy to see all the flowers and enjoy the delicious fragrances as you stroll around an island bed. And finally, with island beds, there is much less lawn to mow.

SELECT A PLEASING SHAPE

The first step is deciding on the shape of your island beds. They can be square, rectangular, circular, oval, or crescent-shaped. I've seen L-shaped and U-shaped island beds, beds shaped like kidney beans, and I've even designed a set of beds in the shape of a giant four-leaf clover. In my own garden, I favor gently curving lines: my outdoor tables and birdbaths are circular; deep S-curves outline many of the borders; and even my new greenhouse is round. Oval, circular, and crescent-shaped island beds that echo other curves are harmonious and unifying.

If your paths and structures flow in straighter lines, you might prefer island beds that are square, rectangular, triangular, or other straight-sided shapes. The more your islands echo the shapes and sizes of adjacent structures, the better they will fit into your garden. But most important, choose whatever shapes please you and create a feeling of well-being. Your garden is the one place in the world where you can make sure that happiness reigns.

MAKE BEDS AT LEAST 8 FT. WIDE

To get enough layers of color and texture into an island, make your beds at least 8 ft. in diameter. This allows you to maintain the plants pretty easily from outside the bed, occasionally stepping in with one foot to reach the plants towards the middle. If your bed is much larger, stepping stones are helpful for traveling inside to weed and groom without compacting the soil.

I learned the hard way that big beds need arterial paths. Without them, the only way I can weed my 14-ft.-deep bed is by trampling plants, hopping on one foot, or walking on my hands. A good idea is to plan your beds with paths as integral parts of the design. In the backyard at the edge of the lawn, I built three concentric, crescent-shaped beds, each 30 ft. long and 6 ft. deep. Bark chip paths run between them. From a distance, all three beds blur together and appear to be one enormously deep border. The paths between them disappear when viewed head-on, yet allow easy access for maintenance and strolling.

In a large garden with ample lawn, I like to group several island beds near each other for greater impact. Three oval islands, 16 ft. long and up to 12 ft. across, make a friendly trio in the lawn between the south side of my house and the grape arbor. They're united by similar shapes and cool color schemes—mainly blue, pink, white, and silver. There's enough space between them to ramble comfortably around

each bed and enjoy the flowers, yet they're close enough to each other to benefit from the repetition of shape and color.

WELL-BEHAVED PLANTS ARE BEST

Unlike traditional borders planted in front of a hedge or fence and viewed from one direction only, island beds are seen from all sides. Choose plants for them with attractive leaves, long flowering seasons, and sturdy legs. In an island bed, you want plants that support themselves without unsightly stakes spoiling the picture.

Just as people living together on an island must learn to get along, plant compatibility is a key to success in island beds. Choose considerate plants that have slow to moderate growth rates—easygoing clumpers that expand gradually from year to year. Avoid rompers like plume poppy (*Macleaya cordata*) that spread by runners, or unrestrained self-sowers like feverfew (*Tanacetum parthenium*)—they will soon become a nuisance, crowding out their shyer neighbors.

To create the strongest impression, focus on one dominant season and choose plants that bloom at that time. Your color will be concen-

Select a shape for your beds. The author prefers gentle curves in her informal garden, but squares and rectangles might be best for a formal garden.

How to Plan an Island Bed Planting

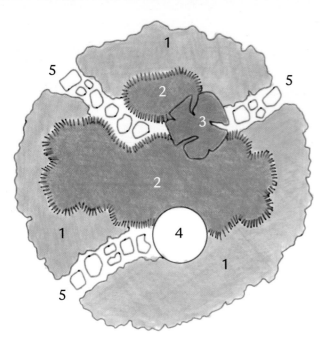

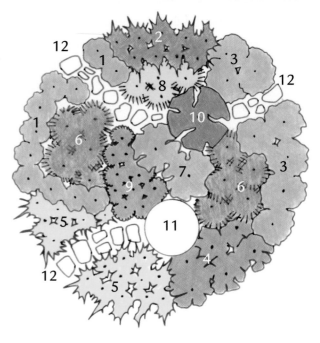

GENERAL PLANTING SCHEME
1 Edging plant
2 Flower filler
3 Tall accent plant
4 Garden ornament
5 Stepping-stone path

DETAILED PLANTING PLAN

1 *Bergenia ciliata*	7 *Gaura lindheimeri*
2 *Sedum spectabile* 'Brilliant'	8 *Lychnis coronaria*
3 *Lavandula angustifolia*	9 *Veronica longifolia*
4 *Geranium macrorrhizum*	10 *Rosa* 'Penelope'
5 *Carex morrowii* 'Variegata'	11 Birdbath
6 *Sidalcea malviflora*	12 Stepping-stone path

Before buying any plants, determine a shape, size, and color scheme for your island bed. Next, sketch a general planting scheme showing edgers, flower fillers, and taller flowers or shrubs. Last, but not least, select the individual plants. For beds more than 8 ft. wide, be sure to include paths that provide access to the center of the bed for chores like pruning and weeding. The bed shown here is 15 ft. wide.

trated like a wonderful fireworks display. Close to the house, plenty of winter color and evergreen foliage keep the blues at bay during a bleak season. The backyard and outlying perimeters of the garden, which you're more likely to visit in mild weather, are more suitable for summer and fall flowers.

If your island bed is large enough, you can include shrubs, perennials, bulbs, and annuals for a diverse display. Shrubs give an island bed some structure and thickness, while perennials contribute interesting foliage and colorful flowers. For the most part, bulbs offer added color, especially in early spring, and annuals are great to fill gaps and extend color into late summer and fall.

PLACE TALL PLANTS IN THE MIDDLE

Since you view an island bed from all directions, it's a lot like looking at a wedding cake. The tallest plants should be at the center, like the top tier of the cake; the shortest plants should be at the edge, like the bottom layer of the cake; and the medium-sized plants are sandwiched in between. Plants don't have to be arranged as carefully as a staircase—but generally keep the taller plants towards the middle of the bed.

To be in good proportion, the height of the tallest plants should be about half the width of your bed—a 5-footer is about tops for a 10-ft.-wide island. Overly tall plants will look gawky and out of scale with their companions. Choose tall plants that maintain their height through most of the growing season and stay away from those that lose height after they bloom. In island beds, *Miscanthus sinensis* 'Morning Light', with slender, luminous, variegated foliage, and the non-invasive white loosestrife (*Lysimachia ephemerum*), with dark, gray-green foliage and pearly-white flower spikes, are both excellent keepers.

If your bed is 15 ft. wide or more, a shrub makes a good accent towards the center of the bed (illustrations, opposite). Choose one that has an attractive form and blooms right along with your perennials. In a shade island bed full of summer color, I've planted summersweet (*Clethra alnifolia*) for its upright shape, handsome leaves, and fragrant, white flowers. In sunnier islands, pink and burgundy tree mallows (*Lavatera* 'Barnsley' and 'Burgundy Wine') make long-blooming centerpieces.

Sometimes it's fun to introduce height with a sundial, birdbath, or piece of sculpture. Occasionally I build teepee trellises and cover them with annual vines like morning glories (*Ipomoea nil* or *I. tricolor* cvs.). These structural elements will help to anchor island beds, which can tend to look a bit adrift in a sea of lawn.

(ABOVE) Give each island bed a color scheme. Lawn serves as a buffer, keeping beds with different colors from looking too busy together.

(LEFT) Birdbaths or sculpture add height and visual interest to beds. Also, use shrubs like this red-twig dogwood to anchor plantings.

EDGE BEDS WITH BOLD-FOLIAGED PLANTS

Edging plants are the finishing touch on an island bed, wrapping them up like ribbon on a package. When beds are surrounded by lawn,

it's crucial to choose edgers with enough height and leaf definition to contrast with grass.

Skip dainty, low-growing perennials such as border pinks (*Dianthus plumarius*), creeping phlox (*Phlox subulata*), and flowering onions

(*Allium neapolitanum* and *A. moly*). They look so much like the lawn that grass seedlings sneak in and camouflage themselves. Instead, choose juicier, bold-leaved perennials that will hold back intruders and declare a clear visual separation from the lawn.

In shade, fragrant masterwort (*Astrantia major*) with handsome, lobed leaves and lacy, cream-colored flowers stands 18 in. tall and blooms nearly all summer and fall. *Heuchera* cultivars like 'Plum Puddin', 'Pewter Veil', 'Chocolate Ruffles', and 'Bressingham Bronze'

have richly colored, maple-shaped leaves and wands of delicate flowers that add to their beauty in late spring and early summer.

In sunny beds, lavender (*Lavandula* spp.) makes a fine, aromatic hedge at the edge of an island. Choose from an abundance of purple-, pink-, and white-flowering forms. Upright sedums also make splendid edgers, especially *Sedum spectabile* 'Carmen' and 'Brilliant', with their succulent, gray-green leaves and thick, showy flower heads.

Well-Behaved Perennials for Island Beds

TALL PLANTS FOR ACCENT
Angel's fishing rod (*Dierama pulcherrimum*)
Culver's root (*Veronicastrum virginicum*)
Cutleaf purple burnet (*Sanguisorba tenuifolia* 'Purpurea')
Fuchsia (*Fuchsia magellanica*, *F.* 'David', *F.* 'Mrs. Popple')
Himalayan honeysuckle (*Leycesteria formosa*)
Loosestrife (*Lysimachia ephemerum*)
Miscanthus sinensis 'Morning Light'
'Penelope' rose (*Rosa* 'Penelope')
Red switch grass (*Panicum virgatum* 'Rehbraun',
    P. v. 'Rostrahlbusch')
Summersweet (*Clethra alnifolia*)
Tree mallow (*Lavatera* 'Barnsley', *L.* 'Burgundy Wine')

FLOWERS FOR FILLERS
Beard-tongue (*Penstemon* spp.)
Checker mallow (*Sidalcea malviflora*)
Frikart's aster (*Aster* × *frikartii*)
Gaura lindheimeri
Hollyhock mallow (*Malva alcea* var. *fastigiata*)
Japanese iris (*Iris ensata*)
Phlomis russeliana
Rose campion (*Lychnis coronaria*)
Russian sage (*Perovskia atriplicifolia*)
Sedum alboroseum 'Mediovariegatum'
Speedwell (*Veronica longifolia*)
Thread-leaved tickseed (*Coreopsis verticillata* 'Zagreb')

BOLD EDGERS FOR LAWN
Bergenia ciliata, *B.* 'Bressingham White',
    B. 'Sunningdale'
Coralbells (*Heuchera* cvs.)
Cranesbill (*Geranium macrorrhizum*, *G. renardii*,
    G. sanguineum var. *striatum*)
Lavender (*Lavandula* spp.)
Lenten rose (*Helleborus orientalis*)
Lungwort (*Pulmonaria* 'Roy Davidson')
Masterwort (*Astrantia major*)
Sedum spectabile 'Carmen', *S. s.* 'Brilliant'
Sweet flag (*Acorus gramineus* 'Ogon')
Variegated sedge (*Carex morrowii* 'Variegata')

DRAPING EDGERS FOR GRAVEL
Border pinks (*Dianthus plumarius*)
Carpathian bellflower (*Campanula carpatica*)
Catmint (*Nepeta* × *faassenii*)
Cinquefoil (*Potentilla nepalensis*, *P. atrosanguinea*)
Cranesbill (*Geranium* × *riversleaianum* 'Mavis Simpson',
    G. × *r.* 'Russell Pritchard', *G. ibericum*)
Deadnettle (*Lamium maculatum* 'White Nancy')
Lady's mantle (*Alchemilla mollis*)
Mexican fleabane (*Erigeron karvinskianus*)
Sedum sieboldii, *S.* 'Ruby Glow', *S.* 'Vera Jameson',
    S. kamtschaticum
Sun rose (*Helianthemum nummularium*)

If your islands are surrounded by gravel or crushed rock, edging plants may spill freely without danger of decapitation by the lawn mower. Border pinks (*Dianthus plumarius*) may billow here, their silver leaves glinting in the sun and spicy-sweet flowers wafting fragrance. This is a great place for the strawberry-shaped leaves of cinquefoils (*Potentilla atrosanguinea*); hardy geraniums (*Geranium* spp. and cvs.), too, offer an abundance of drapers for the edges. In shade or sun, the lobed, green leaves of lady's mantle (*Alchemilla mollis*) catch the morning dew and its chartreuse flowers are compatible with almost every color.

FILL THE MIDDLE WITH FLOWERS

Between the center and edge of an island, foliage is not as crucial as color. Your best bets are perennials and bulbs with long bloom periods. I rely on upright speedwells (*Veronica longifolia*) for spikes of blue-purple flowers that repeat all summer, or as long as I faithfully deadhead. They're enthusiastic about reseeding, so I do have to weed out interlopers. Similarly, rose campion (*Lychnis coronaria*) must be culled out with a firm hand, but its cheerful magenta flowers and gray leaves keep good company with the speedwells and are worth the effort of thinning.

For a touch of buttery yellow in early summer, *Phlomis russeliana* is hard to surpass. Amenable to sun or shade, its ample flowers whorl around sturdy stems in stacked layers. To repeat this pleasing color later in summer, I plant similarly colored daylilies such as *Hemerocallis* 'So Sweet' and 'Suzie Wong'. I like the golden-variegated sedum (*Sedum alboroseum* 'Mediovariegatum') nearby to echo the yellow flowers.

Frikart's aster (*Aster* × *frikartii*) is nearly perfect as a filler. A billowing perennial filled

with blue-violet daisies that flower from summer through fall, it weaves and knits well with companion plants. Russian sage (*Perovskia atriplicifolia*) is another good mid-height perennial, with stems of misty lavender flowers that color up in late summer. The showy spikes of reblooming beard-tongues (*Penstemon* spp.) have captured my heart, and I love them sandwiched towards the front of island beds.

I can't wait to design my next island bed. A collection of new plants sits patiently in their pots on the patio, eagerly awaiting a home. As soon as I decide on a good location and the right shape for a new island bed, they can put their roots down and settle into my garden.

Arterial paths provide access to especially large beds. Even a narrow path makes it easier to tend plants.

DARREL APPS

owns and operates
Woodside Nursery,
where he breeds new
cultivars of daylilies.
His books include the
*Hearst Garden Guide,
Perennials,* and *Stout's
Daylily Book.*

Perennial Border Design *with Foliage*

A mass of 'Silver King'
artemisia brightens up
the whole border with
its silvery foliage.

FOR THE FIRST 30 YEARS I gardened, I had
the wrong idea about how to plant perennial
borders, despite a long career in horticulture. I
always sought out plants because of their flowers, thinking they, and they alone, would make
my garden a sensation. But after years of visiting beautiful
gardens and noticing that the prettiest ones had abundant
foliage plants, I finally learned that it isn't flower color
alone that makes a perennial border a smashing success—
it's the combination of foliage and flowers. This is particularly apparent in monochromatic designs such as the
famous "white" garden at Sissinghurst Castle in England.
At any one time there is very little flower color. What you
see is a carefully orchestrated selection of foliage plants
that range from the deep green of boxwood to the silver-
gray of artemisia. Nowadays, when I design gardens, foliage
is one of my first considerations.

Chrysanthemum pacificum and fennel planted side by side show how leaf texture, shape and color can contrast for a pleasing effect.

Designs that rely heavily on attractive foliage are not limited to traditional borders. Foliage can enhance front-yard cottage gardens, small home-entrance gardens or areas near paths and decks. Any garden can benefit from the long-season interest that foliage gives.

DIVIDE THE BORDER

Over time, I've developed a method for designing perennial borders with foliage plants. I mentally divide the border into front, middle and back sections to help me evenly distribute plants according to certain qualities. I then fill 30% to 50% of each section with perennial plants having reliable season-long foliage displays; this percentage is enough to create a foundation of foliage and still leave room to embellish with flowers.

I often arrange each kind of plant in masses and if the border is a long one, I repeat these groupings down its length for a unified look. If the planting is 10 ft. wide or more, I may include small flowering shrubs and broad-leaved evergreens. The final step is to fill out the bed with flowering plants, but my goal is a border that is attractive even without flowers.

I like to design a border based on a theme. I examine the site, the structures on it and features such as walls, because they often suggest a theme. A border shouldn't have everything tossed into it, so restrict your choices by choosing plants that suit your theme (such as burgundy foliage and flowers) and eliminating others. Expand later when you understand how well the border works for you and what changes might make it more pleasing.

The key to using foliage in the garden is understanding how to select the proper plants. People tend to work the wrong way—they fall in love with a bunch of plants and then they want to bring them all into their garden. Sometimes you just have to ignore some of your own preferences. If you don't know much about a particular plant you want to grow or if you want ideas about the possibilities, visit local nurseries and botanical gardens. You can also read about specific perennials in nursery catalogs or a good reference book. Let's examine one by one the things I consider when choosing foliage plants.

"A border shouldn't have everything tossed into it, so restrict your choices by choosing plants that suit your theme."

USE FORM TO DRAW THE EYE

The overall form of a single foliage plant, as well as its appearance in a mass, is of utmost importance. Some individual plants are wide-spreading mounds, others are narrow columns and still others are fan-shaped. Mounding plants bring your eye down to ground level. Massed, they can provide a horizontal line along which your eye can rest peacefully and look outward for some distance. Epimediums, or *Epimedium* spp., with their medium-textured light or chartreuse foliage, are a good example of mounding plants.

Columnar plants force your eye to rise. Many, but not all, ornamental grasses are columnar. One example is *Panicum virgatum* 'Heavy Metal', a blue-green, thin-bladed grass that grows up to 30 in. tall. Fan-shaped plants are sculptural. Your eye starts to rise, but then the plant fans out, forcing you to stop and look. I plant Siberian iris (*Iris sibirica*) and *Crocosmia* 'Lucifer' for this effect.

A plant's form can even change throughout the year or throughout its life. One form-shifter is *Miscanthus sinensis* 'Gracillimus', a grass with medium green, narrow leaves that grows up to 6 ft. tall when mature. This plant bears brown flower heads at the end of the season. It's a column early in the year, then becomes a fan—a rather large one in some cases.

These three categories don't encompass all plants, but they are useful divisions nonetheless, and you can use them as you plan your border. As a rule of thumb, gradual changes of form from one area of the border to another make a transition more pleasing than rapid shifts do.

TEXTURE AFFECTS PERCEPTION

I think gardeners are accustomed to looking very closely at a plant's leaves when they talk about texture, but an entire plant has an overall texture, too. When I use the word "texture," I'm really referring to both the total plant and to its leaves. Generally, a plant with fine-textured leaves will have a fine overall texture, but there are exceptions. For example, the overall appearance of bear's breeches (*Acanthus spinosus*) is quite bold, yet up close it has a relatively fine texture because of its deeply lobed leaves.

The columnar shape of a mass of porcupine grass at the rear of this border draws the eye upward. Its variegated foliage stands out against the green foliage of the surrounding plants. A grass in the foreground with similar form and texture unifies the design.

This border in Victoria, British Columbia, Canada, shows all the signs of a good design with emphasis on foliage plants. Repetition and variety balance one another to keep the border interesting without becoming a jumble of unrelated plants.

Within a genus, and even a species, there can be considerable variability in texture. Among the artemisias, silver-leaved, mounding perennials I would generally classify as fine-textured, there's a great difference between the lacy, delicate leaves of *Artemisia ludoviciana* and the coarser ones of *A. absinthium* 'Huntington'.

If you're going to use little, airy flowers such as coral bells (*Heuchera* spp.) or meadow rue (*Thalictrum flavum*) to fill the spaces between foliage plants, choose coarse textures as a backdrop. If you're going to use coarser flowers, such as purple coneflowers (*Echinacea purpurea*), plant fine-textured foliage to counterbalance them.

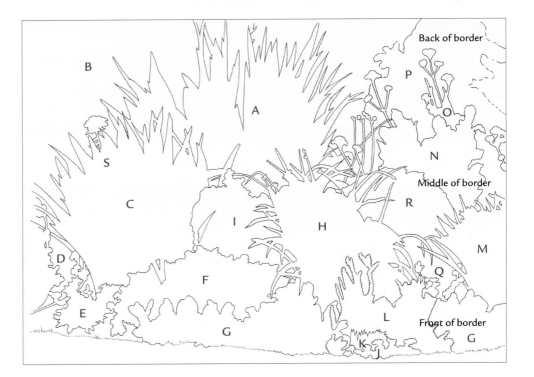

KEY TO PLANTS IN PHOTO AT LEFT

A Montbretia
(*Crocosmia* × 'Lucifer')

B Thoroughwax
(*Bupleurum fruticosum*)

C Montbretia
(*Crocosmia* × 'Spitfire')

D Horehound
(*Marrubium incanum*)

E Goldflower
(*Hypericum* × *moserianum* 'Tricolor')

F Alpine currant
(*Ribes alpinum* 'Aureum')

G Lamb's ears
(*Stachys byzantina* 'Silver Carpet')

H Daylily
(*Hemerocallis dumortieri*)

I Rose
(*Rosa* × *rehderana* 'Katharina Zeimet')

J Lady's mantle
(*Alchemilla conjuncta*)

K Blue-eyed grass
(*Sisyrinchium montanum*)

L Yarrow
(*Achillea* 'Great Expectations')

M Red hot poker
(*Kniphofia* cvs.)

N Great golden knapweed
(*Centaurea macrocephala*)

O Valerian
(*Valeriana phu* 'Aurea')

P Bronze fennel
(*Foeniculum vulgare* 'Purpurascens')

Q Evening primrose (*Oenothera tetragona* var. *fraseri*)

R Euphorbia
(*Euphorbia polychroma*)

S Euphorbia
(*Euphorbia wallichii*)

Similar leaf shapes (sword-like), leaf textures (coarse) and plant shapes (fan) all lend unity to design A, C, H, M

Multi-colored leaves relieve monotony E, F

Use of small shrub with yellow-green foliage and delicate leaf shape F

Height for back of border A, B, P

Coarse flowering plant in front of plant with fine leaf texture O, P

Plants with attractive foliage and flowers A, C, H, J, L, M

Repeated, massed plantings for unity; woolly leaf texture invites touching G

Texture can also affect the way the size of the border is perceived. Finer-textured plants can make a narrow border seem longer by giving the eye plenty of detail to look at. By using bold plants in a large border, you can use fewer plants overall, thereby simplifying the design and making it easier for a viewer to take in.

The style of existing structures can help you decide what kind of texture to emphasize.

For example, a Victorian house with intricate gingerbread trim will mesh best with a border composed of finer-textured plants. On the other hand, bolder textures will probably work better with a contemporary house of glass and wood. Regardless of the style of existing structures, however, you'll frequently want a good share of the plants to be coarse-textured, because these plants will give sub-

The height and the coarse leaf shape of plume poppy, shown at the back of this border, make a good conversation piece. Hollyhock mallow (*Malva alcea* var. *fastigiata*) blooms pink in the foreground.

group together. With a small plant such as *Sedum floriferum* 'Weihenstephaner Gold', one mass might consist of dozens of individual plants. (This sedum is a drought-tolerant, fast-spreading ground cover with green leaves that become bronze in winter and small yellow flowers that mature into crimson seed capsules.) Moreover, I repeat these masses or groups of similar-looking foliage plants several times in a long border. In a short border—say, a space 6 ft. by 12 ft.—there isn't the need, but a longer one is made more cohesive by grouping and repetition.

SHAPE ADDS EXCITEMENT

Different leaf shapes lend excitement to an arrangement of plants. I've discovered that people have a special fondness for heart-shaped foliage. Palmate leaves, which have lobes radiating from a common point, like a palm leaf, are a close second. Whatever leaf shapes you prefer, varying them will draw a visitor down a border to see if any surprises await.

FOLIAGE COLOR CREATES MOOD

It is more difficult for gardeners to accurately remember foliage and flower colors and color combinations than it is for them to remember any other plant characteristic. Ironically, color is the first thing we notice. I've learned that foliage of different colors has different effects, so I try to choose foliage with color in mind. It's like making a quilt—color weaves a pattern, and repetition plays a part in that pattern.

Gray-leaved plants will make an area seem whiter, brighter and cooler. Purple, dark red, bronze and deep green leaves recede into the background and make the border they're planted in seem smaller; in a narrow border they should be used very selectively. Gold-

stance to the design. Ultimately, though, it's the mix of textures that makes a border come together nicely. Choose an assortment of plants with textures from across the range and have fun experimenting with them.

PLANT REPEATING MASSES

Usually, plants make a bigger visual impact when three or more plants of the same species or cultivar are grouped together. Gardeners are often too sparing in the number of plants they leaved plants work best in small numbers as accents.

Variegated plants are most effective when positioned to pick up tones from nearby solid-colored plants. The medium-green leaves and cream variegation of *Phlox paniculata* 'Harlequin' do just that when it is planted next to the green-leaved *Phlox* 'David'. To bring more attention to a variegated plant, set it off by planting it next to black mondo grass (*Ophiopogon planiscapus* 'Nigrescens'), whose nearly black leaves are the perfect foil for the complexity of variegation.

Recently, I worked on a design that included a long walk to an attractive entrance garden. To make the one-acre property seem more like an estate, I wanted the walk to appear longer. Along both sides of it I designed planting strips in which the foliage color changes progressively from dark green at the driveway end to lighter shades of green closer to the door. Because lighter colors make a given space seem larger, the change in colors fostered the illusion of a longer walk.

The quality of a plant's leaf surface can also add drama to a border. Certain hollies have reflective surfaces that can brighten things up a bit. In contrast, meadow rue has plain-surfaced, blue-green leaves that are restful and quieting to the eye. The fuzziness of common lamb's ears (*Stachys byzantina*) invites touching, and the succulence of *Sedum* 'Vera Jameson' is cool and refreshing.

REMOVE UNWANTED FLOWERS

Otherwise-desirable foliage plants can sometimes have significant flowers that change the whole character of the plant—and hence its suitability for a given purpose in a foliage design. Germander (*Teucrium chamaedrys*) is a fine-textured plant often clipped into 6-in. to 8-in. tall hedges and used for edging. However, its effect as an edging plant is destroyed when it puts up flower spikes.

The deep maroon leaves of bugbane (*Cimicifuga ramosa* 'Brunette') provide visual relief from the greens that surround them. Variety and interest result when a wide range of leaf colors is used to good advantage in a border.

This combination of *Crocosmia* 'Lucifer', Japanese blood grass and *Coreopsis grandiflora* is unified by a common leaf shape and hot flower colors, yet shows great variety in the shades of green and red in the leaves. The crocosmia doubles as a foliage and flowering plant.

Luckily, you can often get around the problem by simply cutting off the flowers. Or, just choose a variety that flowers minimally. For example, bear's breeches (*Acanthus spinosus*) are not well suited as foliage plants—it becomes like a piece of art when it blooms because the flower spike is like a carved totem pole; *Acanthvs mollis* 'Latifolius', however, puts on much less of a show.

FINALLY, ADD FLOWERS

When 30% to 50% of the border is filled with foliage plants, I add flowers that will provide color throughout the seasons. I place them so their flower colors complement the leaves of the foliage plants next to them. Here's where it pays to know long-blooming perennials, because they will give you the maximum color effect.

PUTTING THE PRINCIPLES TO WORK

Effective combinations of foliage plants and flowering perennials can be made with as few as two or three plants. As an example, Japanese blood grass (*Imperata cylindrica* 'Red

Barron') offers attractive, red 1-ft.-tall grassy foliage all summer and contrasts nicely with the more upright, green-leaved, gladiolus-like, vertical foliage of *Crocosmia* 'Lucifer'. Add *Coreopsis grandiflora*, with its daisy-shaped yellow flowers and fine, medium green foliage, and you have an attractive composition for a sunny location. The combination is equally pretty in or out of bloom.

A more complex combination uses the tall Joe Pye weed (*Eupatorium fistulosum*) with 'Silver King' artemisia and ground-hugging plumbago (*Ceratostigma plumbaginoides*). The Joe Pye weed is pretty in and out of flower because of its bold leaves on 6-ft.-tall or taller plants, while the 'Silver King' artemisia has silver-gray foliage and flowers that are late and almost inconspicuous. Although slow to start in the spring, the plumbago has blue flowers and fine-textured, plum-colored foliage in the fall. Additional color comes from perennials including purple coneflower (*Echinacea purpurea* 'Bright Star'), mauve daylily (*Hemerocallis* 'Little Grapette'), pink ornamental onion (*Allium* 'Summer Beauty') and pale yellow threadleaf coreopsis (*Coreopsis verticillata* 'Moonbeam').

The process of learning how to employ all these principles to create a harmonious border is very organic. Don't be frustrated with little failures. Even garden designers have to sort things out over time.

ROOM FOR CREATIVITY

The real charm in gardens results when you know the rules well enough to be able to break them to bring out your individuality. If you design only according to a set of rules, the result will be boring. So after you've got everything mapped out, look at your design and knowingly, intentionally, do something "contrary," such as placing a tall plant in the foreground just to break up a monotonous stretch. The result might surprise you.

Don't forget to add at least one plant simply for its boldness or unusual nature. The size and coarseness of plume poppy (*Macleaya cordata*) are startling. It can be 8 ft. tall and 4 ft. to 6 ft. in diameter. A Joe Pye weed (*Eupatorium maculatum* 'Gateway') has huge, salmon-colored flowers and can become absolutely alive with butterflies. Porcupine grass (*Miscanthus sinensis* 'Strictus') and Adam's needle (*Yucca filamentosa* 'Golden Sword') act like exclamation points in the garden by drawing attention to themselves.

Foliage plants are more versatile than you might think. Their potential is limited only by each gardener's imagination. With increased interest in herbaceous perennials in America, it is now possible to find spectacular gardens whose structure is sewn together with carefully chosen foliage. Yours could be one of them.

"Don't be frustrated with little failures. Even garden designers have to sort things out over time."

GREAT
BORDER PLANTS

2

PLANTS ARE THE HEART of beds and borders, whether it's strictly a perennial bed or a mixed herbaceous border. Perennials are the obvious choice for beds and borders, but expansive perennial borders are difficult to maintain. By mixing in flowering shrubs, you can cut down on the number of plants required to fill the border, add greater height and dimension, expand the seasons of interest, and reduce overall maintenance requirements. Annuals also have a place in the border, especially filling in gaps until shrubs and perennials have grown to their mature size.

So we'll take a look at some of the many shrubs that enhance mixed borders, as well as a few other top-performing plants that round out the well-planted garden. You'll learn about some of the best varieties, find out where to place them in a border, and explore ways to mix them with other plants for an eye-catching garden vignette.

SYDNEY EDDISON

teaches gardening at the New York Botanical Garden. The author of four gardening books, including *The Self-Taught Gardener*, she writes for several publications and lectures widely.

Good
Looks
Begin
at the Edge

Edges have a lot of power to draw the eye, so you want to fill them with reliable plants with decorative foliage, such as lamb's ears.

I T MAY BE A SMALL CONTRIBUTION to ornamental horticulture, but I have a theory that if the edges of your perennial borders are crisp and attractive, you are well on the way to a satisfying garden. Well-clad edges create a favorable first impression, reassure garden viewers that all is right with the world, and hide a multitude of sins by diverting attention from weeds or other flaws in the background.

Think of edges as lines that delineate shapes and, at the same time, define adjoining spaces. The edge that contains flower bed also outlines the shape of the adjacent lawn, path, or ground cover, like the dividing line in the yin-and-yang symbol. Edges create order. They set apart the man-made from the wild and divide space within a garden. They also frame pictures, direct the eye, and provide unity. From a design point of view, they even determine style. Rectilinear edges bespeak formality; and curving edges, informality.

All's well in a bed when the edges are tidy. Silvery-leaved lamb's ears and yellow 'Moonbeam' coreopsis both make good edging plants because they keep their neat appearance over a long season.

The key to an effective edge for your perennial border is suitable plant material. In order to trace a clear-cut line, you need a tidy, good-looking, self-supporting plant that is highly tolerant of local climatic conditions. Finding perennials that fulfill the many obligations of an edging plant is a challenge. Because so much is expected of them, their numbers are limited, and you have to experiment. You don't really know a plant until you grow it for a few seasons and see how it performs. But to get you started, I've put together a sampler of appealing, well-behaved edgers for a variety of situations.

ONLY THE MOST RELIABLE BELONG OUT FRONT

You need a plant that will emerge from winter dormancy with vigor and become mature relatively quickly. A slow developer will leave a gap and interrupt the line of the bed. Most important of all, edgers must have decorative, disease-free, and insect-resistant foliage that retains its color and carriage throughout the growing season.

The foliage requirement is a tall order for flowering plants, which usually go through an ugly phase. Take bearded irises: so handsome in May with their swordlike leaves; so miserable in July when borers leave their blades in tatters. After flowering, even stalwart daylilies lose their charm as the leaves turn yellow. In the middle of a large, mixed border, foliage defects may go unnoticed, but up front and center, they show. For this reason, foliage plants star as edgers. And those with colored leaves really give flowering plants a run for their money.

However, if you are content only with flowers, select those that have comparatively good foliage and boast either a long season of bloom or repeated periods of bloom. Remember that the flowers must not disfigure the plant in their passing, and if shearing after bloom is necessary, select a plant that covers the evidence with new growth.

Height and size are the final considerations in selecting edgers. Keep in mind the dimensions of the bed and the scale of the garden as a whole. My perennial border is 100 ft. long and 12 to 15 ft. wide. It is viewed from a distance and demands big plants in order to fit into its setting of woodland and overgrown cow pasture. I use 2-ft.-tall *Sedum* 'Autumn Joy' as an edger because it's in proportion with the rest of the plants and with the background. It also measures up in terms of all-season demeanor and excellent foliage. However, a lower-growing sedum such as 'Ruby Glow' would be more suitable for a smaller garden.

clears away the rotted leaves and gives new ones a chance to fill in the gaps.

In most gardening books, the flowers of lamb's ears are criticized for their magenta color and small size. Indeed, they are tiny and deeply imbedded in the thick silver-white fuzz that clothes the 12-in. to 18-in. flower stalks, but I like them. For a couple of weeks, they give the flat ribbon outlining the border another dimension. If you don't want flowers, there is a sterile cultivar called 'Silver Carpet', which is something of a misnomer because the leaves are more gray-green than silver. The large-leaved 'Helene von Stein', which is very bold and handsome, also has gray-green foliage.

Native from the Caucasus to Iran, lamb's ears spreads rapidly and self-sows where it is happy. While it prefers full sun, it will grow in partial shade. It's only strict requirement is good drainage. It will rot in standing water and resents high humidity. Otherwise, it is everything an edger should be: easy to grow, tolerant of some extremes in temperature (USDA Hardiness Zones 4 to 10), and presentable over the long haul.

SOFT, SILVERY LAMB'S EARS ARE HARD TO BEAT

Lamb's ears, or *Stachys byzantina*, is my all-time favorite edging plant. This lovely, mat-forming plant has long, elliptical leaves as white as fleece and thickly covered in silky hairs. My perennial bed, which lies at the foot of an east-facing slope, is bordered with them. They flow northward in a silver stream below the retaining wall, curving gently in and out as the border follows the contours of the hillside. They tie the garden together and look bright and beautiful for eight months of the year, longer in a dry, snowless winter. For a brief period in early spring, the previous year's foliage looks awful, but a vigorous raking

LILYTURF FOR YEAR-ROUND FOLIAGE AND FALL BLOOM

Variegated lilyturf (*Liriope muscari* 'Variegata'), which grows well in Zones 5 to 10, is my next favorite edging plant. In some respects, lilyturf is superior to lamb's ears as an edger because it remains good-looking nearly all year and grows in either sun or shade. Admittedly, variegated

Choose an edger with a long season of bloom. This catmint started blooming in early spring, came back for a midsummer flush, and put out flowers once more in the fall.

Plants with colored foliage make eye-catching edgers. Look beyond green foliage and you'll find attractive edgers like *Heuchera americana* 'Pewter Veil', which has a dense, neat habit.

forms bleach out in intense sunlight, but given a little afternoon shade, their yellow- and green-striped foliage is beyond compare.

The slightly blunt, arching blades of lilyturf measure ½ in. wide and make neat, grassy tufts about a foot high. The clumps increase generously but do not spread, and they are easy to divide in spring. The narrow spikes of lavender-blue flowers resemble attenuated grape hyacinths, which accounts for lilyturf's species name *muscari* (grape hyacinths belong to the genus *Muscari*). The flowers in early fall add to their value because most perennials are through blooming by then.

TWO EASY EDGERS WITH SUMMER FLOWERS

I am partial to catmints (*Nepeta* spp.) and threadleaf coreopsis (*Coreopsis verticillata*) for summer-flowering edgers in beds with full sun. These plants are of easy culture, are possessed of worthwhile foliage, and flower over a long period. Most catmints thrive in Zones 3 to 10, coreopsis in Zones 4 to 10.

Catmint's small, upright, lavender-blue flower clusters appear with the tulips in early spring and go on unabated until about mid-June. At that time, they begin to sprawl, and I shear them. Within a week or two, new foliage begins to appear, and they bloom again—a less impressive flush in midsummer, and then another in the fall. The last hurrah is almost as full and long-lasting as the first. In between, soft mops of gray-green foliage decorate the front of the border.

The coreopsis blooms for so long the first time that it can be forgiven for taking a rest afterward. Hundreds of small, yellow, daisylike flowers completely cover the dense network of dainty stems and leaves. When the blooms are spent, they aren't unattractive. They look like little buttons. Cut the whole plant back by about a third with scissors when the buttons are more numerous than the flowers. The sheared foliage is neat and unobtrusive.

MAGNIFICENT FOLIAGE THAT THRIVES IN THE SHADE

As our garden boasts 11 mature maple trees and is surrounded by forest, shade is a fact of life. If you have a similar situation, don't be dismayed. The genus *Hosta* alone offers dozens of small-leaved cultivars to furnish the edge of a woodland path or tree-shaded border. Hosta gets four stars for magnificent foliage, which comes in shades of green, blue, and gold. Hostas thrive in Zones 4 to 9 and like soil rich

in organic matter, though they will make do in average soil.

'Hadspen Blue' and 'Blue Cadet' have wonderful frosty blue-green leaves and form dense, low mounds of overlapping leaves. 'Gold Edger' has heart-shaped, bright chartreuse to gold leaves and develops into a neat, 10-in., dome-shaped clump. Nifty little 'Kabitan' has narrow, pointed, yellow leaves with wavy edges trimmed in dark green. 'Golden Tiara' is fast growing to about a foot by 16 in. and has small, heart-shaped, or cordate, leaves. Green forms abound, and the species *H. tardiflora* is one of the best with very dark green leaves.

Generally, the white or lavender flowers of hostas are disappointing in appearance, though often sweetly scented. The spikes of

To edge a shady bed, the overlapping leaves of hostas won't disappoint.

drooping bells start to bloom from the bottom up, and the spent blossoms detract from those that are opening. However, some cultivars have better flowers than others. Those of *H. tardiflora* are exceptional. The spikes are crowded with lavender bells and are very decorative.

TWO DELICATE EDGERS FOR SHADY BEDS

As neat edgers for shady areas, epimediums run hostas a close second. These deceptively delicate-looking plants tolerate dry shade with equanimity and provide charming spring flowers, as well as lovely foliage. Before the leaves unfurl, thin stems arise, carrying airy sprays of spidery blossoms in rose-pink, yellow, or white. In mild climates, epimediums keep their leaves almost all winter. They grow in Zones 5 to 8.

Epimedium grandiflorum has two popular cultivars, both desirable: 'Rose Queen' and 'White Queen'. The species *E. × rubrum* has crimson flowers, and a cultivar of *E. versicolor* called 'Sulphureum' comes in yellow. While the flowers are delightful close up, they are not showy, except en masse. However, the foliage that follows is outstanding for its elegance. Branched stems displaying angel-wing leaflets form graceful mounds. *E. × rubrum* has particularly fetching leaves, red-veined and often flushed with red at the edges. In the fall, they assume shades of red and bronze, and cling to the stems until December.

Without knowing anything about it, I once bought a tiny pot of *Vancouveria hexandra* from a North American Rock Garden Society plant sale. I have since come to delight in this

Out front, reliable foliage is better than fleeting flowers. 'Helen von Stein' lamb's ears looks vibrant spring through fall in Martha McKern's Connecticut garden.

graceful cousin of epimedium as a lacy edging for large-leaved hostas. The white flowers of vancouveria are so minute that they really don't count, though if you examine them carefully, their shape is intriguing. They are called "inside-out flowers" for their reflexed sepals, which look as if the wind has blown them backward.

Delicate, compound foliage is vancouveria's greatest asset. The individual leaflets are small, rounded, or lobed, and about ¾ in. across on wiry, threadlike stems. Indigenous to the moist woods of the Pacific Northwest, this engaging plant is surprisingly tolerant of dry shade and surprisingly hardy as well. I can vouch for vancouveria in my Zone 6 garden, and I can still recall carpets of it at Millstream, the memorable woodland garden created by H. Lincoln Foster and his wife, Timmy, in chilly Litchfield County, Connecticut (Zone 5).

SOLUTIONS FOR MOIST SOIL

Lady's mantle (*Alchemilla mollis*), hardy from Zones 3 to 8, is a beautiful edger for rich, moist soil and partial shade. While it tends to look shabby in my dry perennial border, it thrives in my friend Martha McKeon's border and looks lovely combined with hostas. The silvery, sea-green leaves are palmate and precisely pleated. In the morning they catch the dew, each one supporting a tiny crystal ball. Frothy, chartreuse flowers are an added attraction in early summer. Cut the flowers and leaves down when they begin to look messy. New foliage will soon fill in.

Coralbell hybrids (*Heuchera* × *brizoides*) are another of Martha's most successful edging plants. They grow happily in either full sun or part shade, but they need moisture-retentive soil to perform well. In suitable soil, these coralbells favor the gardener with masses of tiny, bell-shaped flowers in loose sprays at the

top of fine, but sturdy, 2-ft. stalks. These stand above neat clumps of rounded, scalloped leaves. The flower colors run the gamut of pinks, reds, and white, with many named cultivars. Most were developed in England by Alan Bloom from the native American species *H. sanguinea, H. micrantha,* and *H. americana.*

Today, new selections are being made here with the emphasis on foliage. *H. americana* 'Montrose Ruby' has stunning, dark-red foliage; 'Pewter Veil' is a knockout with silver-frosted red leaves; and *H. micrantha* var. *diversifolia* 'Palace Purple' is deservedly popular for its rich red-purple leaves. All the coral bells are well-behaved edgers, which grow in Zones 3 to 9.

For good-looking foliage year-round, try variegated lilyturf as an edger.

"The genus Hosta *alone offers dozens of small-leaved cultivars to furnish the edge of a woodland path or tree-shaded border."*

ERICA GLASENER

is a contributing editor for *Fine Gardening* and the host of HGTV's *A Gardener's Diary*. She was previously in charge of the educational program at the Scott Arboretum of Swarthmore College.

Flowering Shrubs Enhance
Mixed Borders

Lilac-blue, spiky flowers bloom all summer long on chaste tree's gray-green foliage. This sun-lover will grow into a small tree.

WHEN I STARTED gardening, I planted mostly spring- and summer-flowering perennials. But between bursts of bloom, the garden looked lackluster. Then, as fall turned to winter and my herbaceous plants died back, the garden suddenly seemed desolate. At this point, I realized that adding shrubs would anchor the garden from season to season and provide a beautiful backdrop for my splashier perennials and annuals.

Traditionally, shrubs have been segregated from the flower garden and used as foundation plants near the house or as specimens in the middle of the lawn. When they're planted in a bed, it's usually with others of the same type. By integrating these trustworthy beauties in an herbaceous border, you can highlight the best traits of many plants and create year-round interest. Even small gardens can be enhanced with the addition of shrubs.

While I'm fond of shrubs with beautiful flowers, I also want them to flourish without a lot of special attention, to resist pest and disease problems, and to look attractive even when not in bloom. Some of my favorites are evergreen, while others are deciduous with colorful dormant twigs or bark. I also select both spring- and summer-blooming shrubs to ensure a succession of showiness. My favorite flowering shrubs include the viburnums, as well as many old-fashioned shrubs, such as beautybush, pearlbush, and golden St. John's wort. These have all been used in gardens for a long time—and for good reason.

THESE SPRING-BLOOMING SHRUBS SPARKLE

Just when it seems that spring will never arrive, Japanese kerria (*Kerria japonica*) lights up the garden with bright-yellow blooms. A tough, twiggy shrub, kerria has dense, bright-green stems which stand out in winter. Unlike most flowering shrubs, kerria will grow and bloom in full sun or almost-full shade. In warm climates its flowers last longer if protected from the hot, afternoon sun. If it's planted in well-drained soil and if the dead wood is pruned annually, kerria will thrive year after year. I prefer the elegant simplicity of the single-flowered cultivar 'Shannon' to the double-flowered 'Pleniflora', but both reliably enhance a border.

Slender deutzia (*Deutzia gracilis*) is another good performer that requires little care.

Tall and arching, butterfly bush makes a reliable anchor in a border. Its flowers attract hordes of butterflies during its long bloom time in summer.

Though dwarf cultivars are available, I recommend the species if space allows. This stalwart shrub produces masses of beautiful, white flowers in spring that last for weeks. While you don't need to prune it often, periodic thinning of dead branches will maintain its graceful, arching form. Plant it in the middle or back of the border and take advantage of the shade it creates by underplanting it with evergreen ground covers like bugleweed (*Ajuga reptans*) or small hostas such as *Hosta venusta*.

Another old-fashioned favorite of mine is pearlbush (*Exochorda racemosa*). It produces buds 1 to 2 in. wide that look like clusters of pearls at the end of the branches. In early spring, the buds open to become masses of white flowers. Underplanted with early bulbs, such as miniature daffodils and irises, pearlbush creates an enchanting picture. Give this tough shrub room to grow, since it can reach 10 ft. or taller.

Beautybush (*Kolkwitzia amabilis*) also ranks high on my list. Its bell-shaped flowers, pink with a yellow throat, appear in mid-spring. When it finishes flowering, the seedheads dry on the tips of the branches, reminding me of furry little creatures. When not in bloom, beautybush is a fountain of dark-green foliage, and an ideal backdrop for smaller shrubs or for perennials like purple coneflowers (*Echinacea purpurea*) and black-eyed Susans (*Rudbeckia hirta*).

A spring standout, Chinese snowball viburnum (*Viburnum macrocephalum*) should be

'Pink Cloud' beautybush produces abundant pink blooms. Its dark-green foliage forms a handsome backdrop for smaller shrubs and perennials.

Golden St. John's wort shines in the middle of a border. Its bright-yellow flowers stand out against bluish-green leaves.

reserved for larger gardens. While some consider it too big and gaudy, I think you get a lot for your money with this shrub. It makes a large exclamation point in the garden, with the blossoms weighing down the branches. When Chinese snowball viburnum first blooms, its flower clusters start out chartreuse. Then, as they get bigger, sometimes up to 8 in. wide, they turn pure white. It's as if you get two different bloom periods. The dark-green leaves are semi-evergreen in southern states, where it can grow to 20 ft. high and 15 ft. wide. For a dramatic white garden, I like to combine Chinese snowball viburnum, slender deutzia, and white foxgloves (*Digitalis purpurea* 'Alba') with white-flowering pinks (*Dianthus* spp.) as edging.

SUMMER-BLOOMING SHRUBS MAKE COLORFUL COMPANIONS IN BORDERS

A reliable summer bloomer is butterfly bush (*Buddleia davidii*) and its many cultivars and hybrids. This sun-lover comes in hues from pure white to deepest purple. From midsummer until frost, butterfly bush earns its name as hordes of winged beauties flit from flower to flower in search of nectar. It makes a fine companion for purple coneflowers, Mexican sage (*Salvia leucantha*) or 'Powis Castle' artemisia (*Artemisia* 'Powis Castle'). Depending on growing conditions, butterfly bush can reach 10 ft. high and wide in a single growing season. However, dwarf varieties, like 'Nanho Blue' or 'Petite Plum', grow to only 4 or 5 ft.

(ABOVE) Bold blooms of Chinese snowball viburnum start out chartreuese and gradually turn white. This sprawling shrub needs room to spread its branches.

(LEFT) Beautybush's pink-and-yellow bell-shaped blooms look stunning for several weeks in spring.

Flowering Shrubs Enhance *Mixed Borders* | 53

Another favorite of butterflies, chaste tree (*Vitex agnuscastus*) is a small tree valued for its summer blooms and finely dissected foliage. It can grow to 20 ft. in southern climates, but in colder areas may reach only 8 to 10 ft. Its gray-green leaves set off the spiky, lilac-blue flowers that bloom June through September, especially with deadheading. Plant it next to butterfly bush or with blue salvia (*Salvia farinacea* 'Victoria') and lamb's ear (*Stachys byzantina*).

A drought-tolerant shrub that shines year-round is golden St. John's wort (Hypericum frondosum 'Sunburst'). It offers bright-yellow flowers reminiscent of powder puffs. In winter, I appreciate its reddish-brown, peeling bark and handsome, blue-green foliage, which is mostly evergreen. Growing 3 ft. tall to 4 ft. wide, this St. John's wort makes a wonderful accent in the middle of a border along with summer-blooming perennials like white gaura (*Gaura lindheimeri*), or *Salvia guaranitica*, which produces electric-blue flowers late in the season.

"Butterfly bush earns its name as hordes of winged beauties flit from flower to flower in search of nectar."

Shrubs That Shine in Borders

NAME	DESCRIPTION	CULTURE
Beautybush *Kolkwitzia amabilis*	Large, upright, vase-shaped; 6 to 10 ft. tall, slightly less across; pink flowers with yellow throat	Full sun or light shade; well-drained, average soil; Zones 5 to 9
Butterfly bush *Buddleia davidii*	Large, upright, open; to 10 ft. high and wide; honey-scented flowers, in colors including lavender, white, yellow, deep-purple, burgundy, and pink	Full sun; prefers well-drained, fertile soil; Zones 6 to 9
Chaste tree *Vitex agnus-castus*	Large, upright, and wide; can grow to become a tree from 10 to 20 ft. tall; aromatic, blue-green foliage; lilac-blue flowers	Full sun; prefers moist, loose, well-drained soil; Zones 6 to 9
Chinese snowball viburnum *Viburnum macrocephalum*	Large, upright, and rounded; 10 to 20 ft. high and up to 15 ft. wide; flowers start out chartreuse and gradually turn pure white	Full sun to partial shade; well-drained soil; Zones 7 to 9
Golden St. John's wort *Hypericum frondosum*	Small, upright; to 3 ft. high and 4 ft. wide; handsome reddish brown, peeling bark; bright yellow flowers	Full sun to partial shade; well-drained, average garden soil; Zones 6 to 8; excels in the Midwest
Japanese kerria *Kerria japonica*	Upright, dense, and twiggy mound; 3 to 6 ft. tall and 6 to 9 ft. wide; bright green stems stand out in winter; yellow flowers	Full sun to almost-full shade; well-drained, average soil; Zones 4 to 9
Pearlbush *Exochorda racemosa*	Upright, open, spreading; 10 to 15 ft. high and wide; white flowers	Full sun or light shade; well-drained, loamy, acidic soil; Zones 5 to 9
Slender deutzia *Deutzia gracilis*	Small mound with a graceful, arching form; 2 to 4 ft. high and 3 to 4 ft. wide; white flowers	Full sun or light shade; moderately fertile soil; Zones 5 to 8

ELISABETH SHELDON

is the author of *A Proper Garden* and *The Flamboyant Garden.* She is a frequent garden lecturer and previously ran a small nursery specializing in perennials and herbs.

Annuals
Pep Up Perennial
Borders

(LEFT) Some annuals make thrilling combinations by themselves. Red fountain grass and silvery plectranthus complement each other and look at home among perennials.

(INSET) The foliage of 'Plum Parfait' coleus serves as a foil for Japanese forest grass.

I THINK OF MYSELF as a purist, so when I started my perennial border some years ago, I wanted nothing but perennials. After all, I reasoned, a perennial border should contain only perennials, shouldn't it? But, as time went by, I added several compatible shrubs to my garden and began calling it a mixed border. That new definition liberated me to add a few annuals. Even so, I felt a lot less conscience-stricken when I learned I wasn't the first to use annuals in a perennial border. My gardening betters had paved the way long ago.

Ever since the introduction of the herbaceous border in the days when William Robinson and Gertrude Jekyll ruled most of the known horticultural world, it has been considered legal to fill in gaps in a perennial or mixed border with annuals. It is almost inevitable that dull areas—and even blank, empty spots—will occur in a perennial border as the summer wears on. Perennials with nothing to contribute but their blooms stop blooming. Then, there

57

"I comb through seed and plant catalogs to find new candidates and old favorites."

are those perennials that are subject to unsightly afflictions if the summer is too wet—or too dry.

Even when you carefully orchestrate the garden so that delicious combinations of color and texture will provide an ever-delightful symphony from early spring to late autumn, those annoying gaps will occur. Perhaps rabbits ate the blue star (*Amsonia tabernaemontana*) or deer the delphinium. Maybe the wildly changing spring weather did in some of the roses. Whatever the cause, your symphony has been deprived of important notes and, in some cases, whole themes. It's then that you need annuals.

(RIGHT) Annuals can do more than fill gaps in mixed borders. Using those with subtle colors and beautiful form makes annuals an integral part of the garden's design.

(OPPOSITE) Silvery licorice plant looks good with almost anything. The author planted some next to a dark-foliaged snapdragon.

SUBTLE ANNUALS LOOK RIGHT AT HOME IN BORDERS

Annuals, yes, but not just any old annuals. The solution won't be found, unless you are amazingly lucky, in a few six-packs from your local garden center. Most annuals raised for "the trade" are bred for maximum impact. They are, shall we say, "assertive." Their bold reds, bouncy yellows, and bright oranges are rarely compatible with the soft pastels of a typical perennial garden.

Instead, I look for annuals with more refined hues and, if possible, delicate—or, at least, attractive—foliage. These kinds of annuals are rarely found in garden centers, so I comb through seed and plant catalogs to find new candidates and old favorites, then raise those that I can from seed in early spring under lights. There are countless annuals to choose from, but I'll discuss those I've grown and used in my own garden.

BLEND YELLOWS AND BLUES INTO THE BORDER

One of the best annuals I've found for blending with other yellows in a border is a chrysanthemum, *C. coronarium* 'Primrose Gem', a 12- to 15-in.-tall plant with lacy foliage whose upright stems hold corymbs of small, soft yellow, semidouble daisies with gold centers. Fresh and lovely, they help carry the garden through the dog days of August. It's hard to find a perennial with which it doesn't harmonize.

Another yellow jewel is the Mexican tulip poppy (*Hunnemannia fumariifolia*). It's not a very pale yellow, but the effect of its elegantly cut, silver leaves and its 3-in., silky cups glistening in the sunlight is one of delicacy and grace. Members of the poppy family don't like to be moved, so plant their seeds in peat pots

The bluest blues belong to gentian sage. The author loves its color enough to devote a special part of the border to showcasing this tender perennial, which she grows as an annual.

or directly in the ground early in May. Thin young plants to stand 7 to 8 in. apart.

Some blue annuals also look stunning and blend well in perennial borders. One spring I planted a flat of sky-blue Chinese forget-me-nots (*Cynoglossum amabile*). Their gray-green leaves and clouds of tiny, cobalt flowers were such a joy that I saved the seed and sprinkled it along the front of the border in the fall. The plants kept coming up all the next summer.

More and more salvias are finding their way into borders, and with good reason. I'm thinking of tender perennials or annuals such as blue salvia (*Salvia farinacea*), a perennial in USDA Hardiness Zone 8 and south, but an annual in my Zone 5 garden. This branching, 18-in. plant bears never-ending spikes of purple-blue flowers. There are several named varieties, but the best of the lot is 'Victoria'. Every year I also plant seed of gentian sage (*S. patens*), perhaps the bluest flower around. Even though it's not hardy here and I have to gather seeds every autumn, gentian sage has earned a reserved section in my garden.

Other cooperative subjects that I've discovered include bachelor's button (*Centaurea cyanus*); *Tweedia caerulea*, with its cerulean stars; and love-in-a-mist (*Nigella damascena*).

SOME ANNUALS ARE BEST AT THE EDGE OF THE BORDER

Pinks (*Dianthus* spp.) shine at the very edge of the garden. You can find the cushion or taller (12- to 15-in.), tufted sorts in white, pink, and rose, either solids or bicolors, with either green or silvery, blue-gray foliage. Nearly all of them have a spicy fragrance. I think that the best cultivars are from the Ideal and Telstar series. They bloom in the first year from seed but behave otherwise like proper—though rather tender—biennials. They should get through at least a second season in areas where winters are not very severe. You can get seeds for separate colors. This summer I'm trying 'Ideal Crimson' and 'Telstar Dark Purple'.

Having been dazzled by the sight of a sea of blue pimpernels (*Anagallis monellii*) growing gloriously among the gray rocks of the Kabylie

Mountains in Algeria, I once tried them on the edge of my border. That summer we broke records for heat, humidity, and drought and my poor pimpernels pined away and died. However, they are most desirable plants, especially for gardeners searching for pure blue. A perennial in Zone 7 and south, it makes a 9-in. mound that will sit chummily among your clumps of pinks.

GREAT FOLIAGE EARNS THESE ANNUALS THEIR PLACE

Annuals with good foliage contribute a lot to the perennial garden. I've devoted one section of my border to combinations of dark burgundy-red and chartreuse. I used a ruby-foliaged Japanese barberry (*Berberis thunbergii* 'Atropurpurea Nana'), and the lovely Japanese forest grass (*Hakonechloa macra* 'Aureola'), and enriched the area with annuals including a few sumptuous new coleus (*Solenostemon* spp.)—wine-colored ones such as velvety 'Plum Parfait' and 'Mars', a globe-shaped plant with short, maroon leaves. Coleus have come a long way since your grandmother grew those awful red and green things on her windowsill.

I had another new thrill when I planted a clump of non-hardy red fountain grass (*Pennisetum setaceum* 'Rubrum') against the wonderful gray *Plectranthus argentatus*, actually a shrub that is hardy in Zone 10. When the grass produced its fluffy, buff-colored flowers, and the tender perennial *Salvia microphylla* 'Trinidad Pink' on its right covered itself with small rosy blossoms, I thought that I'd been very clever indeed. I shouldn't have been so smug—I failed to give the plectranthus enough room and it squashed another salvia completely. It needs an area 2½ ft. tall and wide.

I also used licorice plant (*Helichrysum petiolare*) last summer. The ordinary silver one, placed in the front of the border, made a stunning companion for a dark-foliaged snapdragon (*Antirrhinum majus* 'Black Prince').

ANNUALS LOOK BEST AS PART OF A REPEATING THEME

The real challenge of using these temporary tenants of the perennial border is placing them effectively in established plantings. I try to combine color, form, and texture of both annuals and perennials felicitously, keeping in mind rule number one of any successful composition, whether it's a novel, a painting, a piece of music, or a garden—repetition of theme.

I site plants so that the eye of the observer, as it travels through the garden, can pick up recurring themes—even though they might be provided by different plants. Above all, I try to weave annuals in and out of the perennials so that the annuals repeat their own colors as well as those of the permanent border residents. For example, I might place several 'Primrose Gem' chrysanthemums at mid-border, to repeat the color of some pale yellow daylilies farther back, or use rosy pink *Salvia viridis* to echo the hue of Japanese anemones. That's how it works. Instead of plunking down a bunch of petunias and marigolds into the empty spots in your garden, you first evaluate what is there already, then search out plants that look as if they belong. If you're successful, they'll have every appearance of having been part of the plan from the beginning.

"Annuals with good foliage contribute a lot to the perennial garden."

FRANCES WENNER

is a garden designer, lecturer, and writer who has been gardening for more than 25 years. She writes a local gardening column and lectures regularly for several horticultural organizations.

Lacing *the Border with* Beauty

(CLOCKWISE FROM TOP LEFT) Baby's breath, goatsbeard, dead nettle, and love-in-a-mist all add a lacy texture to the garden.

LIKE MANY GARDENERS, I longed for lush banks of greenery and plush borders overflowing with foliage and flowers. Yet, once achieved, my garden cried out for a lighter touch—something to brighten those heavy masses of color. In a way, it was much like a bold expanse of solid-colored fabric seeking a finishing touch of trim. So, just as a seamstress might turn to lace—that most ephemeral of fabrics—I turned to plants with filigreed foliage and delicate flowers. I call these plants "garden laces."

With their finely threaded or patterned forms, garden laces add glamor, elegance, and lightness to the garden tapestry. Brooding assemblies of evergreens can be thrown into relief by a single specimen of the wedding cake tree (*Cornus controversa* 'Variegata'). Bold, structural border plantings can be tied up with a ribbon of silver mound (*Artemisia schmidtiana*) or threads of sweet alyssum (*Lobularia maritima*). Lacy plants also contrast with and

Greater masterwort *(Astrantia major* spp. *involucrata* 'Margery Fish') sports lacy, white flowers with pink centers.

Japanese maples are noted for their lacy, finely dissected foliage, which is colorful in both spring and fall.

highlight other plants in garden groupings. Tulips and alliums in spring; iris, peonies, and poppies in early summer; daylilies and hostas as the season progresses—they all benefit from the gossamer touch of garden laces.

TRIMMING WITH LACE

The most common use of lace—both with fabric and in the garden—is trimming or edging. Such lacy edgings are particularly useful where the area to be set off contains flowers, foliage, or hardscaping materials that give a solid or bold impression, rather than those involving "busier" schemes. A trail of sweet alyssum fronting a dark-leaved border of peonies will be far more effective than this same edging combined with the multicolored blossoms of petunias. Smooth stone and brickwork practically demand the lightening touch of garden laces. Suitable edging plants include filigreed artemisias, crisply cut bloody cranesbill (*Geranium sanguineum* var. *striatum*), hazy love-in-a-mist (*Nigella damascena*), and tiny laced flowers—such as thread-leaved coreopsis (*Coreopsis verticillata* 'Moonbeam') or 'Lemon Gem' marigold (*Tagetes* 'Lemon Gem').

One of my favorite combinations for a shady spot is bleeding heart (*Dicentra eximia* 'Alba') setting off hostas and hellebores. Flowering all summer, the bleeding heart highlights one of my garden's darkest corners.

LOVELY SWATCHES OF LACE

Insets—swatches of lace used to break up and complement surrounding flowery fabrics—emphasize the depth and solidity of their neighbors that, in turn, highlight the airy quality of the lace. Laces also add depth to plantings, as the eye can pierce them, discerning patterns of light and darkness. They cast their ornamental shadows upon broader-leaved neighbors, adding texture to once-smooth surfaces. Baby's breath (*Gypsophila paniculata*), bishop's flower (*Ammi majus*), cosmos (*Cosmos bipinnatus*), boltonia (*Boltonia asteroides*), and fennel (*Foeniculum vulgare*) are among the many useful inset plants.

One of my favorite inset combinations positions the exquisite lace blooms of bishop's flower against the deep red and purple foliage of barberry, the brilliant red blooms of rose-mallow (*Hibiscus moscheutos* 'Lord Baltimore') and clumps of red-leafed canna. In another border, maidenhair ferns (*Adiantum pedatum*) mingle delicately with clumps of golden 'August Moon' hosta, a pairing edged with spiraling sweet woodruff (*Galium odoratum*).

VEILS OF GAUZY GARDEN LACE

Just as a lace veil evokes mystery and romance, garden veils drop their gauzy curtains before us, raising curiosity about partly obscured plants and encouraging us to explore scantily hidden spaces. Plants used as veils also add height throughout the garden, thus breaking the monotonous, stair-step quality of so many traditional borders.

Spiky yuccas pierce veils of soft Russian sage (*Perovskia atriplicifolia*), while statuesque and silky maroon hollyhocks (*Alcea rosea* cvs.) peek through clouds of white crambe (*Crambe cordifolia*). Tall verbena (*Verbena bonariensis*), bush clovers (*Lespedeza* spp.), and fennel all make excellent garden veils. Many ornamental grasses also make superb veils. In my garden, giant feather grass (*Stipa gigantea*) drapes across a path, forcing sensory contact, while fountains of *Miscanthus sinensis* plumes allow glimpses of the prickly limbs of Scotch thistle (*Onopordum acanthium*). Elsewhere, the deep-toned foliage and pale lemon umbels of

Artemisia ludoviciana 'Silver Queen' adds a silvery, lacy touch to borders all season long.

"Garden veils drop their gauzy curtains before us, raising curiosity about partly obscured plants."

bronze fennel (*F. vulgare* 'Purpureum') screen the David Austin rose 'Othello' and silky 'Caroline' hibiscus.

LACE-PATTERNED FOLIAGE

Like a fabric upon which lacy patterns are drawn or painted, certain plants with solid leaves are overlaid with lacy patterns. Admired for their intricate design, these lace-patterned plants invite us to look more closely. Here, the pattern is not offset by air or emptiness, but rather by the deep green background of the leaf. This contrast exudes a crispness in character. Milk thistle (*Silybum marianum*), dead nettle (*Lamium maculatum*), and coralbells (*Heuchera* spp.) display this lacy overlay.

Accent your perennial border with a cluster of lacy flowers such as bishop's flower.

SELECT LACES FOR COLOR AND SEASON OF BLOOM

Choosing garden laces begins with contemplation and observation. Where are the dark corners or heavy areas of the garden? Which broad-leaved plants could use a lift? Where could a lacy edging enhance a scene? Should laces be scattered about the garden or concentrated in an area or two?

Once you know where lacy plants could accent your garden, consider your options for color and season of bloom. Dusty-pink hairy chervil (*Chaerophyllum hirsutum*) is delightful with blue-leaved hostas; but with clear, red roses, it only succeeds in looking muddy. Similarly, dead nettle cascading over gray stone

might be just the thing, while this same plant rambling among variegated hosta would look hopelessly jumbled. While white laces conjure up images of bridal purity, blues and purples evoke impressionist paintings, and dusky reds create a somber or richly elegant mood.

Selecting laces for season of bloom is also important. Paired with the giant blossoms of purple alliums (*Allium giganteum* and *A.* 'Globemaster'), flowering white crambe sparkles elegantly. Sweet cicely (*Myrrhis odorata*) will tuck its white froth around the feet of felted mulleins (*Verbascum* spp.), but will have gone to seed before nearby lilies can open their heavy-headed buds.

A Selection of Lacy Garden Plants

ANNUALS AND TENDER PERENNIALS

Ammi majus (bishop's flower)

Tagetes 'Lemon Gem' (marigold)

Cosmos bipinnatus (cosmos)

Euphorbia marginata (snow-on-the-mountain)

Gypsophila elegans (baby's breath)

Lobularia maritima (sweet alyssum)

Myrrhis odorata (sweet cicely)

Nigella damascena (love-in-a-mist)

Silybum marianum (milk thistle)

Verbena bonariensis (tall verbena)

PERENNIALS AND BIENNIALS

Adiantum pedatum (maidenhair fern)

Alcea rosea cvs. (hollyhocks)

Anchusa azurea (blue bugloss)

Arabis spp. (rock cress)

Artemisia spp. and cvs.

Aruncus dioicus (goatsbeard)

Astrantia major (greater masterwort)

Boltonia asteroides (boltonia)

Brunnera macrophylla (bugloss)

Calamintha grandiflora 'Variegata' (variegated calamint)

Chaerophyllum hirsutum (hairychervil)

Coreopsis verticillata 'Moonbeam'
   (thread-leaved coreopsis)

Corydalis lutea (corydalis)

Crambe cordifolia (white crambe)

Crambe maritima (sea kale)

Dianthus spp. (pinks)

Dicentra spp. (bleeding hearts)

Euphorbia corollata (wild spurge)

Foeniculum vulgare (fennel)

Galium odoratum (sweet woodruff)

Geranium sanguineum var. *striatum* (bloody cranesbill)

Gypsophila paniculata (baby's breath)

Lamium maculatum (dead nettle)

Lespedeza spp. (bush clovers)

Limonium latifolia (sea lavender)

Michauxia campanuloides

Myosotis scorpioides (forget-me-nots)

Osmunda regalis (royal fern)

Perovskia atriplicifolia (Russian sage)

GRASSES, SHRUBS AND TREES

Acer palmatum cvs. (Japanese maples)

Aralia elata (Japanese angelica)

Caryopteris × *clandonensis* (bluemist shrub)

Cornus controversa 'Variegata' (wedding cake tree)

Miscanthus sinensis cvs. (eulalia)

Stipa gigantea (giant feather grass)

As insets, ferns add depth to border plantings like this one with bloody cranesbill and variegated hosta.

The lacy, silver foliage of 'Huntington' artemisia shines among rose campion and 'Homestead Purple' verbena.

A SPECIAL SPOT FOR YOUR GARDEN LACES

Lacy plants have many homes in the garden. You might confine them to shaded areas where their airiness is appreciated. Containers flanking a doorway are another good spot, as they can effectively screen and enhance architectural elements. A shady spot in a rock garden might sport a patch of royal fern (*Osmunda regalis*), and wild spurge (*Euphorbia corollata*) could grace the entry to a sunny pergola.

For a change of pace, try a border of laces featuring a season-long display of feathery foliage and flowers interspersed with a few, slightly more substantial companions. A froth of azure forget-me-nots (*Myosotis scorpioides*) could be interplanted with an early, yellow tulip like 'West Point'. This might be followed by clumps of snow-on-the-mountain (*Euphorbia marginata*), sea hollies (*Eryngium alpinum*), artemisias, and yarrows (*Achillea* spp.), followed later by Russian sage, tall verbena, and blue mist shrub (*Caryopteris* × *clandonensis*). In a reverse approach, more substantial

Soften hard surfaces with garden laces. This maidenhair fern adds a light touch to a stone foundation.

The delicate leaves of this Japanese maple stand out against the solid, colorful blossoms of an azalea.

perennials—such as black-eyed Susans (*Rudbeckia* spp.) and chrysanthemums—could add depth, while mulleins or evergreens tie down the border at each end. Spikes of feathery goatsbeard (*Aruncus dioicus*) could add vertical contrast and creamy color to this combination. Amid a carpet of green, a circular bed of pinks (*Dianthus* spp.) would look like a large lace doily flung down upon the lawn.

A border of laces requires careful siting. In addition to adequate sunlight, lacy plants need a solid background to set off their diaphanous quality. A hedge, wall, or other dark backdrop will allow a mass planting of lacy plants to be seen to their best advantage. Protection from the afternoon sun will keep these fine-textured plants from "frying" in summer's heat, as will frequent attention to watering needs. Such a border will grow in loveliness as the plants fill out and spread their feathery wings.

"Lacy plants need a solid background to set off their diaphanous quality."

ELISABETH SHELDON

is the author of *A Proper Garden* and *The Flamboyant Garden*. She is a frequent garden lecturer and previously ran a small nursery specializing in perennials and herbs.

Shrubs
for the Perennial
Border

Spiraea japonica 'Alpina' will continue to flower until fall if deadheaded. Its height of only 12 in. makes it a handsome addition to the front or middle of the mixed border.

I N THE 19TH CENTURY, when money and space were no problem for most leisure-class landowners and skilled labor was readily available, herbaceous flower borders were planted with perennials only—masses of them. Today, many garden lovers have found that the so-called mixed border is more practical than the herbaceous perennial border of the past.

In a mixed border, compatible shrubs mingle with herbaceous perennial plants. Because shrubs are woody and don't die back to the ground in winter, they add structure to the garden year round, unlike perennials. Also, since shrubs don't need dividing, spraying, staking or cutting back (except, perhaps, for an occasional pruning), they save time and labor.

Twenty or so years ago, I started digging and planting my long mixed border here in upstate New York. Back then, I included many shrubs, some of which I had to remove later and replace with more appropriate subjects.

Potentilla fruticosa 'Abbotswood' brightens the border from June until frost. This long-blooming shrub grows to 2 ft. or 3 ft. tall and is easily contained by clipping.

Since digging up shrubs is neither fun nor easy, gardeners who are contemplating including them in their perennial borders or island beds should think carefully before they begin, and perhaps avoid making some of the mistakes I made.

CHOOSING SHRUBS WISELY

Not every shrub is a good candidate for the mixed border. A suitable choice should have certain qualities: It should be deciduous and proportionately sized to the perennials; have no colonizing instincts, underground stolons, or swiftly multiplying suckers; and bear handsome foliage and flowers.

Border shrubs must not become so large that they crowd out perennials. A 10-ft. by 10-ft. beautybush (*Kolkwitzia amabilis*), for example, won't leave room for many perenni-als. Also beware of overly vigorous shrubs like *Stephanandra* species, a fiend that uses every foul device known to the plant kingdom to take over the earth. It will even develop roots where branch tips touch the ground, like a wild bramble. Beware of forsythias, too. They can make an instant jungle by means of new shoots and tip rooting. Finally, use caution with big, old-fashioned lilacs (*Syringa vulgaris*), whose matted surface roots deplete the soil around them of all moisture and nourishment.

The type of shrub you need should have handsome foliage and flowers that are of a size and color that will combine well with perennial flowers and not overpower them. For instance, it's the rare perennial garden that could serenely accept the presence of some of the strident flower colors of hibiscus and modern azaleas.

SPIREAS FEATURE DELICATE FOLIAGE AND FRAGILE FLOWERS

There are some lovely dwarf spireas whose slender leaves and fragile-looking flowers go perfectly with perennials. I have been growing and enjoying a little *Spiraea lemoinei* I got many

"For me, the fine texture of ornamental grasses is the perfect complement to perennials and roses."

(FAR LEFT) Kerrias are prized more for their foliage than their flowers. The flowers appear only for a few weeks in spring, but the variegated foliage lasts for the rest of the season.

(LEFT) *Caryopteris* × *clandonensis* 'Blue Mist' adds a haze of blue to the August garden, providing a cool foil for sedums and other fall perennials.

years ago. It does sucker, but it is not too hard to control. Because *S.* × *bumalda* remains at a height of around 2 ft. to 3 ft., it is quite satisfactory in the border; but now I'm trying some new spireas. One of the prettiest is *S. bullata,* a 15-in.-tall native of Japan whose dark, leathery, 1¼-in.-long blue-green leaves are quite attractive even without the deep rose flower clusters it produces in July. This little shrub doesn't have the loose, arching habit of many of its better-known relatives but holds its branches quite upright. Gray-leaved plants such as lavender and some of the small artemisias, if planted nearby, would bring out the fine color in the leaves and flowers of *S. bullata.*

Several years ago, my decision to order *Spiraea japonica* 'Alpina' for my mixed border made me aware of the sad state of confusion that surrounds spireas. I received one plant labeled *S. japonica* 'Alpina' from three different nurseries. They are now all of different heights and have different growth habits. One that has reached only 10 in. is probably the true 'Alpina', since it is spreading out along the

ground (as it is supposed to do) rather than growing up. Catalogs and reference books disagree as to what its ultimate dimensions should be, but the authority I trust the most says 12 in. tall by 30 in. wide. True *S. japonica* 'Alpina' starts producing clusters of pink flowers in late June and will keep on producing them until fall if deadheaded. It makes a good front-of-the-border, or better yet, edge-of-the-woods garden plant; small bulbs could live happily among its low, slender, trailing branches.

Another spirea in my garden is *S. nipponica* 'Snowmound', a 4- to 5-ft.-tall, upright specimen whose small blunt leaves are dark blue-green and very attractive. As you may have surmised from the name, its flowers are pure white. You could use this as a shrub almost anywhere, including the back of a large border—perhaps combined with shrub roses.

There are lots of 2-ft. to 3-ft.-tall spireas with variegated foliage in yellow, copper and orange, but I feel that they would look inappropriate in the usual pastel perennial border.

A slow-growing and graceful shrub, *Deutzia gracilis* 'Nikko' presents its snow white flowers in spring. Under-planted here with bugleweed *(Ajusa reptans)*, deutzia is hardy to Zone 5 with protection.

a shrub with white flowers, 'Abbotswood' can't be beat, with its little gray-green leaves and snowy white blossoms. It blooms over such a long period that the flowers are a real contribution in maintaining a flowering border. I have it near the pale yellow 'Wisley Primrose' helianthemum, another helianthemum with white flowers, a white single peony with gold stamens, and a pale yellow Ghent hybrid azalea. Now I want *P. fruticosa* 'Gold Star' to finish the composition; it has the largest, most elegant, back-curving, pale yellow blossoms I've seen on a potentilla.

DEUTZIAS ARE WELL BEHAVED

I keep meaning to put some of the small deutzias in the border. They have excellent foliage and no unneighborly tendencies, and seem to answer the job requirements for a mixed-border shrub. They're low, neat, and refined—not greedy, not raucous. *Deutzia gracilis* is a slender, graceful, 2-ft. to 4-ft.-tall Japanese shrub that has narrow, pale green, alternate leaves and produces trusses of single white or pink scentless flowers in late May. I do have several of the new import *D. crenata* 'Nikko' in the sunnier section of my woods garden. They are really unusual little creatures. Mine, in their third year, are about 4 in. tall and 12 in. wide, but they will grow to 2 ft. by 5 ft. eventually. My catalog says that 'Nikko' is cold hardy to USDA Hardiness Zone 6, but mine show no sign of suffering in my Zone 5 garden. I cover them well with evergreen boughs in winter, looking forward to their pure white flowers in spring.

I'm thinking of ordering the 4-ft. to 5-ft.-tall *D.* × *elegantissima* 'Rosealind' for the center of a large loop in my border. It's a deutzia from Ireland that has deep rose blossoms in June and should be hardy.

POTENTILLAS HAVE AN ARCHING FORM

The 2- to 3-ft.-tall potentillas are excellent for mixed borders; their branches arch out over their neighbors, but a simple clipping will keep them from doing harm. My favorite was *P. fruticosa* 'Abbotswood' until I saw *P. fruticosa* 'Gold Star'. Actually, if you are looking for

GROW KERRIA FOR THE FOLIAGE

Another shrub for the mixed border is Kerria—not, however, the common one, *Kerria japonica* 'Pleniflora', whose dark green leaves and double, bright yellow flowers don't blend well with most perennials. Choose, instead, *K. japonica* 'Picta' (also known as 'Variegata'). This cultivar has yellow flowers, but they are single, delicate little things floating (for only two weeks) on a haze of pale green and white produced by slender variegated leaves on long green branches. It grows only to 2 ft. or 3 ft. tall and is very nice.

LILACS ADD A FRAGRANT TOUCH

Try small Korean lilacs (*Syringa palibiniana*, or *S. meyeri* 'Palibin') with perennials. They might take up a lot of moisture and nourishment, but one could combine them with lavender, perennial salvias (*Salvia nemerosa*, or *S. × superba*) or yarrows (*Achillea* spp.) that don't require as much food and drink. These 5-ft.- to 6-ft.-tall lilacs are wonderful shrubs with very small leaves that do not mildew in summer and turn a nice pinkish beige in fall. Their little trusses of lavender-pink blossoms, which appear a week or so after ordinary lilacs finish blooming, are wildly fragrant.

Another good choice is *Syringa patula* 'Miss Kim', which is even shorter than the Korean lilacs and has inflorescences bearing pink buds and "icy lavender" blossoms.

BLUE MIST SHRUB HAS GRAYISH LEAVES

The last and possibly the loveliest shrub I have to suggest is the 3-ft.-tall, August-blooming blue mist shrub (*Caryopteris × clandonensis*). Of all the cultivars of caryopteris available, I especially like 'Dark Knight', though I admit I haven't seen them all by any means. The one I most often see planted, and have seen swarming all over gardens in Hamilton, Ontario, where it seeds itself, is 'Blue Mist'. This one has gray, pointed, opposite leaves; fuzzy, delicate, powdery lavender-blue flowers; and a rather unrestrained way of floating its branches about. It grows 2½ ft. to 3 ft tall. I prefer 'Dark Knight', which has a more definite upright shape, deeper green-gray leaves with gray undersides, and darker violet-blue flowers than 'Blue Mist'. I obtained a nice little specimen last spring that has already grown to its full height of 3 ft. It gave me such pleasure, especially while it was blooming with *Sedum* 'Autumn Joy' and *Lespedeza* 'Pink Fountain', that I'm going to tuck it well in for the winter and order three more.

Small lilacs, unlike large varieties, can be good neighbors in the mixed border. 'Miss Kim' grows to be no more than 6 ft. tall and is delightfully fragrant.

Well-Placed Shrubs

Make Borders Better

MARIETTA O'BYRNE

and her husband, Ernie, own Northwest Garden Nursery in Eugene, Oregon, which specializes in perennials. Marietta lectures and teaches on various areas of gardening.

In summer, borders billow with flowering perennials while a few well-placed dogwoods add structure and colorful foliage. In winter, the shrubs' berries and bright branches will continue to provide visual interest.

I N JUNE THE PERENNIAL BORDER is a billowing mass of color—the glory of the summer garden. But by August plants begin to flounder, and by fall the border is in disarray. Come winter, after cleanup, the beds are bare. The billowing mass has gone dormant to slumber below ground until the next season.

But a few well-placed shrubs can give a border structure and an aspect of permanence year round. I think of shrubs as the spine and bones that hold the soft body of flowers together. Well-chosen shrubs integrate with perennials and add interest for more than just one short season. Not only do they add support for lax perennials in late summer but they also give definition to the whole bed throughout the year. Though shrubs take longer to reach maturity, their striking foliage, pretty flowers, and graceful forms and shapes expand the depth of beauty our gardens have to offer.

AVOID SHRUBS THAT AREN'T GOOD MINGLERS

The prospect of planting a big, long border can be daunting. My first attempt was 10 years ago, with a freshly tilled bed measuring 100 ft. long by 12 ft. to 15 ft. wide. When it came time to plant, I placed big pots and sticks as markers to visualize mature shrub specimens in various spots. I recognized that shrubs did not need to be confined to a straight line at the back of the bed, serving only as a background. I wanted smaller shrubs to step forward, backed by larger ones. And I knew still smaller shrubs could be dotted along the front or used as focal points at the edges of the bed.

I chose shrubs that I consider good minglers, like *Weigela* and *Deutzia*, with shapes that reach out to or cascade through perennials. I passed on others that are not happy cohorts in a mixed border. Rhododendrons, for example, are not good minglers, with their rounded, very self-contained shapes. Conifers are also bad candidates, unless they're used as a background hedge and kept at a slight distance from leaning perennials. Though some of their shapes and needle foliage contrast wonderfully with broad-leaved perennials, conifers flinch at the friendly embrace of herbaceous companions. Any part of a conifer that is covered for a summer by perennial foliage dies, leaving big, brown, ugly holes and scars on the shrub. Conifers do better in close companionship with very short perennials, grasses, and heathers.

CHOOSE SHRUBS THAT PROMISE YEAR-LONG INTEREST

The ideal shrub for the mixed border has exceptional foliage—deep green, purple, gold, silver, or even variegated. Its leaves may be glossy or soft and furry to the touch. Light may dance through filigreed leaves. Colorful veins may mark its foliage. This endless variation holds your interest throughout the seasons, and complements perennial companions.

And, of course, the ideal shrub has flowers. They may be late-blooming to liven up the border during the tired end-of-summer days, or early-blooming to add excitement to a border just bursting in spring. Flower color is another consideration in working shrubs into a planting scheme. White is a good and safe choice, especially as a backdrop, as it harmonizes with all other colors. Pink can be nice, especially in spring before the onslaught of the hot oranges and reds of late summer. Consider also the mellow blues of hydrangeas (*Hydrangea* spp.) and rose of Sharon (*Hibiscus syriacus*)—blues of the sky on a lazy, late summer day. What could be more satisfying?

Naturally, the ideal shrub exudes a heavenly (though not heavy) fragrance that's fruity, but not too sweet. It's a fragrance that makes you stop in mid-stride and turn around, just for the pleasure of inhaling it again. For me, the winner in this category is 'Guincho Purple' elderberry (*Sambucus nigra* 'Guincho Purple').

In fall, colorful leaves cover the ideal shrub before carpeting the ground. And in winter its

"I choose shrubs that I consider good minglers, with shapes that reach out to or cascade through perennials."

Exceptional Shrubs for the Mixed Border

NAME	HEIGHT	ZONES	INTEREST
Background and Mid-Border Shrubs			
Cornus alba cultivars (red twig dogwood)*	8–10 ft.	2 to 7	Variegated or golden foliage; red winter branches
Cornus stolonifera cultivars (red osier dogwood)*	7–9 ft.	2 to 7	Variegated foliage; red or yellow winter branches
Cotinus coggygria 'Velvet Cloak' and 'Royal Purple' (smokebush)*	10–15 ft.	5 to 8	Dark purple foliage
Deutzia 'Mont Rose' and 'Magicien'	4–5 ft.	6 to 8	Pink spring flowers; graceful, arching habit
Heptacodium miconioides (seven-son flower)	20 ft.	6 to 9	Fragrant, creamy white summer flowers; attractive peeling bark
Hydrangea aspera ssp. *villosa*	4–12 ft.	7 to 9	Late-summer blue flowers
Physocarpus opulifolius 'Dart's Gold' and 'Diabolo' (ninebark)*	7–10 ft.	2 to 7	Golden or dark purple foliage, white flowers in spring
Pyrus salicifolia 'Pendula' (willow-leaf weeping pear)	10–15 ft.	4 to 7	Silver-gray leaves; elegant, drooping branches
Rosa glauca	5–7 ft.	2 to 8	Pink flowers; bluish foliage; red hips
Sambucus nigra 'Guincho Purple' (purple-leaved elder)*	10–15 ft.	6 to 8	Fragrant spring flowers; purple foliage; graceful, arching habit when mature
Sambucus racemosa 'Plumosa Aurea' and 'Sutherland Gold' (cut-leaved European red elder)*	8–10 ft.	3 to 7	Finely cut, golden leaves
Viburnum macrocephalum (Chinese snowball viburnum)	15 ft.	6 to 9	White flowers in spring, fading to buff seedheads
Viburnum plicatum var. *tomentosum* 'Summer Snowflake' (doublefile viburnum)	8–10 ft.	5 to 8	Bright white lace-cap flowers summer through fall
Viburnum sargentii 'Onondaga' and 'Susquehanna' (Sargent viburnum)	6–12 ft.	3 to 7	Dark green or maroon-tinged foliage; late-spring flowers; bright red winter fruit
Weigela 'Looymansii Aurea' and *W. florida* 'White Knight' and 'Wine and Roses'	4–6 ft.	5 to 8	Golden or purple foliage; late-spring pink or white flowers
Focal Point Shrubs			
Berberis thunbergii 'Helmond Pillar' (Japanese barberry)	4–5 ft.	4 to 8	Upright form; reddish, purple leaves
Buxus sempervirens 'Graham Blandy' (boxwood)	4–6 ft.	6 to 8	Narrow, upright habit
Buxus microphylla cvs. (littleleaf boxwood)	3–4 ft.	6 to 9	Dense, rounded shape
Ilex crenata 'Sky Pencil' (Japanese holly)	4 ft.	6 to 8	Extremely narrow, columnar form
Lonicera nitida 'Baggesen's Gold' (boxleaf honeysuckle)	4–6 ft.	7 to 9	Golden foliage; may be trained into upright shapes
Front-of-the-Border Shrubs			
Berberis thunbergii 'Atropurpurea Nana', 'Aurea', and 'Bagatelle' (Japanese barberry)	1–4 ft.	4 to 8	Golden or purple foliage; dense, rounded form
Caryopteris × *clandonensis* 'Worcester Gold' (blue mist shrub)	2–4 ft.	6 to 9	Golden foliage; late-summer lavender flowers
Hypericum androsaemum 'Albury Purple' (tutsan)	2–3 ft.	6 to 8	Purple-tinged leaves; yellow summer flowers; red berries
Spiraea japonica cvs. (Japanese spiraea)	1–4 ft.	4 to 9	Golden foliage; pink spring flowers
Symphoricarpos orbiculatus 'Foliis Variegatis' (coralberry)	2–5 ft.	2 to 7	Yellow-edged variegated leaves

Prune hard in late winter to control height in mid-border positions.

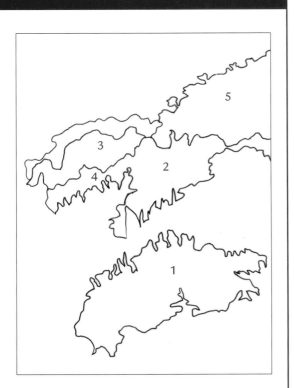

Shrubs occupy front, middle, and back positions in this lush border.

Berberis thunbergii 'Atropurpurea Nana' (**1**) sits in front where its dark foliage complements red astilbe flowers and heuchera leaves.

In a mid-border spot, 'Velvet Cloak' smokebush (**2**) has been pruned to encourage vigorous foliage growth, adding a rich swath of deep, dark purple.

Back-of-the-border shrubs include *Deutzia* 'Mont Rose' (**3**), *Hydrangea arborescens* (**4**), and *Sambucus racemosa* 'Plumosa Aurea' (**5**). In addition to their beautiful flowers and foliage, they provide support for tall perennials like foxglove and meadow rue.

gnarled, colorful branches and bright berries provide relief from the winter doldrums.

I know of no shrub in my earthly life that fulfills all of these conditions, though some do come close. So before that impulse buy at the local nursery, ask yourself what promises any potential shrub purchase holds for the full year. If two weeks of pretty flowers is all it offers, if the shrub has a tendency toward blackspot, or if it's an uninteresting blob shape the rest of the year, leave it on the nursery bench for a less discerning customer.

LIMB UP BACKGROUND SHRUBS

If you plan to use a shrub as a backdrop, carefully consider its ultimate size. To be effective, especially in a wide border, it needs to stand above the tallest plant placed in front of it. In general, shrubs that grow to 10 ft. make good backdrops. As the shrub matures, you can prune out its lower limbs, in effect turning it into a small, multi-trunked tree. Many of the taller shrubs, such as purple-foliaged 'Guincho Purple' elderberry, late-flowering seven-son flower (*Heptacodium miconioides*), or silvery willow-leaved pear (*Pyrus salicifolia*), lend themselves well to this treatment.

Nature abhors a vacuum, so before weeds have a chance to grow, I fill the bare earth beneath a limbed up shrub with new perennials. I choose tall, lanky, flowering plants that like the shrub's filtered shade at their feet and appreciate its upper limbs for support. Yunnan meadow rue (*Thalictrum delavayi*), with its frothy white or lavender flowers, or any of the taller bellfowers (*Campanula* spp.), weaving through the shrub's foliage, make it appear to magically rebloom at various times in the summer. Clematis vines are also perfect

> *"If you want to convey a forceful message, shrubs can quite literally take on the shape of exclamation points."*

mates for barelegged shrubs, twining around their legs and peeping out among the upper branches.

GIVE BEDS SOLIDITY WITH MID-BORDER SHRUBS

Island beds are a challenge to plant because they are viewed from all sides and must be pleasing from any angle. Towering perennials, such as delphiniums, look impressive in June as center focal points, but leave gaping holes in August. Alternatively, shrubs dotted throughout the length of the bed give a much more solid and permanent look. Here I may plant a strongly variegated shrub or one with colored foliage. But moderation is advised—too much variegation results in a busy buzz. For mid-border plants, I love the various forms of red-

and yellow-twig dogwood (*Cornus alba* and *C. stolonifera* cvs.). They come with yellow, purple, and variegated leaves and have glowing red or yellow bare branches in winter. In addition, they are amenable to pruning and shaping any time of year. Clematis, honeysuckle, or hardy geraniums love to gambol among their branches.

Rosa glauca, with its bluish foliage, light pink flowers, and purple-red hips is another versatile shrub for mid-border placement. Color combination possibilities are endless. It looks somber in early summer with 'Patty's Plum' poppy (*Papaver orientale* 'Patty's Plum') and red masterwort (*Astrantia major*). Rosa glauca also shines in a silvery-blue border underplanted with wild rye grass (*Elymus magellanica*). It does very well in sun or part shade without growing lanky.

Choose shrubs that are good minglers, like *Weigela* 'Looymansii Aurea'. Its arching branches, covered in soft pink flowers and chartreuse leaves, embrace the blue flowers of *Geranium pratense*.

USE SHRUBS AS FOCAL POINTS

If you want to convey a forceful message, shrubs can quite literally take on the shape of exclamation points. They shout, "Stop your eye here!" "This is the end of the bed!" "Here is the path!" A clipped shrub forces the eye to rest and stands out like a sentinel among the frothy, undulating mass of undisciplined summer perennial growth. 'Graham Blandy' boxwood (*Buxus sempervirens* 'Graham Blandy'), for example, grows into a slender, tall column and needs little shearing.

An electric shrub in a shady border, *Berberis thunbergii* 'Aurea' glows when surrounded by deep green ferns, hellebores, and hostas.

Besides traditional clipped boxwood shapes, fast-growing 'Baggesen's Gold' boxleaf honeysuckle (*Lonicera nitida* 'Baggesen's Gold') can be clipped into obelisks, balls, or other shapes in-between. For a more club-shaped upright form in purple tones, there is 'Helmond Pillar' barberry (*Berberis thunbergii* 'Helmond Pillar').

PLACE SMALL SHRUBS UP FRONT

Small shrubs toward the front of the border can take the place of perennials. Again, I tend to put the most emphasis here on foliage. Good-looking foliage shines from spring to fall, while perennials and annuals go through their ups and downs. Because shrubs are so noticeable when planted up front and center, their time of flowering and flower color are also critical considerations. For example, the purple-green foliage of *Hypericum androsaemum* 'Albury Purple' blends well with any color at the front of a border. But its midsummer yellow flowers and red berries would certainly look better in the company of deep red dahlias or yellow crocosmias than among bright pink phlox.

Allow for a little looseness in your perennial border. The general rule of big plants in back, small plants in front doesn't have to be followed rigidly. A little variation in height, with medium-sized shrubs dotted along the front

Placed strategically at the end of a bed or a path, a shrub can communicate, "Stop here!" as does the dark purple, upright form of 'Helmond Pillar' barberry.

SHAPE SHRUBS GENTLY AND SPREAD COMPOST IN WINTER

Wading through a sea of perennials in July or August with a backpack sprayer on or lugging out a container full of prunings can wreak havoc in a border. For this reason, I don't use butterfly bushes (*Buddleja davidii* spp.) as background shrubs. I find their brown seedheads unattractive, and I don't want to trample the garden to deadhead them weekly. The rounded seedheads of hydrangeas, on the other hand, can wait until winter to be clipped back and they look lovely in the fall. Roses that have a tendency toward blackspot are best kept where they can be sprayed easily or, better yet, ripped out altogether.

Tempted by a lovely photo or description in a mailorder catalog, you envision a handsome specimen delivered to your doorstep, only to have the mailman bring you a tender shrublet that's at best 10 in. tall. Instead of keeping a new little shrub in a pot for three years, I plant it out in its designated spot when it's about 1 ft. tall, and then surround it with a cage or grow-through support. This keeps perennials from smothering the little shrub, and often hurries it into faster growth to reach lighter regions. Once the tables are turned and a shrub threatens to smother surrounding perennials, you can either prune it up or dig and move the perennials.

Large shrubs like *Deutzia*, some *Viburnum* species, *Physocarpus opulifolius*, and elder-

and middle, makes a border much more interesting. Your eye will follow the undulations in height and observe greater detail. In a very even composition, the eye tends to skim over the whole and miss much of the fascinating and beautiful detail that makes a border a work of art.

"You've got to feed your shrubs if you want them to grow into big, beautiful specimens."

berries are ungainly in youth. They persist in shooting 5-ft.-long whips straight into the air—like teenagers, they don't know what to do with all of their energy. Certainly, shape them a bit, but don't be too harsh. The long whips will be next year's flowering stems, and the weight of blooms will bend the branches down into a graceful, pendulous arch.

A different pruning method applies when all you want is a crop of new, vigorous foliage. Because the deepest colored leaves on a smokebush (*Cotinus coggygria*) are on the new shoots, you need to employ a ruthless pruning method called stooling. In late winter or early spring, cut the shrub down to about 2 ft. from the ground. It will easily put on 4 ft. of new, lush foliage growth by summer, but it will have no flowers. This technique can also be used on willows (*Salix* spp.) and red- and yellow-twig dogwoods.

Finally, I must preach the gospel of compost. Plants can never have too much of it, so don't be stingy. You've got to feed your shrubs if you want them to grow into big, beautiful specimens; compost also cuts down on the watering. I have never met a shrub that disliked a yearly measure of compost applied around its roots in winter. Perennials like their measure of compost, too, and pushing all those wheelbarrow loads around will keep you equally strong and healthy—for all the years it takes to watch your young shrubs grow to splendid maturity.

A nearly perfect shrub, 'Guincho Purple' elderberry has fragrant while flowers in spring, rich burgundy foliage, and a graceful growth habit.

JUDITH C. McKEON

is a professional gardener, lecturer, and leader of garden tours. She consults for her business, The Garden Advisor, and is the author of *The Encyclopedia of Roses* and *Gardening with Roses*.

Roses Enliven

a Border

Purple foliage and flowers form a rich background for roses. The white blooms of the rugosa rose 'Blanc Double de Coubert' glow against purple-leaved smokebush and the lavender-blue flowers of catmint (*Nepeta* 'Six Hills Giant').

PRIZED FOR THEIR BLOOMS and scent, and feared for their reputation for disease, roses inspire mixed feelings. Gardeners typically plant roses in single-species rows or ban them altogether. I've discovered there's a compromise.

At the Morris Arboretum at the University of Pennsylvania in Philadelphia, where I'm chief horticulturist, we've planted many roses in unconventional ways. When shrub roses are grown as graceful specimens in the mixed border, they become part of its architecture, giving structure and a substantial backdrop for perennial companions. Like other ornamental deciduous shrubs, roses enhance the garden with seasonal interest of their flowers, foliage texture and fruit displays.

Shrub roses come in a variety of habits and sizes, from low foreground shrubs to large, princely specimens for the back of the border. Shrub roses contribute a romantic accent to the garden, but they also thrive in harsh sites,

Vining perennials inter-mingle artfully with roses. A purple-flowered clematis (*Clematis* 'Jackmanii') clambers through the shrub rose 'Gertrude Jekyll'. White-flowered valerian (*Centranthus ruber* 'Albus') skirts the combination.

including sand dunes, rock outcroppings and roadsides.

A glance through a rose catalog can be confusing because roses are classified by their ancestry. But the classification matters less than their attributes. I'll discuss some of the best roses from a number of classes, new and old, and describe some of our most successful perennial companion plantings.

Sun-loving perennials—the most beautiful and effective partners for these iron-clad roses—fall into various categories: those with blue flowers such as catmint; those with tall flower spikes such as red hot pokers; those with globe-shaped flowers such as alliums; those with silver or red leaves; and those with a lax, spreading habit such as hardy geraniums that allows them to conceal a rose's naked ankles.

ONCE-BLOOMING ANTIQUE ROSES BLOSSOM HEAVILY

A decade ago, gardeners had to search aggressively for antique roses, but today they can be easily obtained. Some aristocratic antique roses bloom only once in the season, usually for several weeks in June, providing enormous quantities of blossoms. The best make beautiful garden pictures draped with clematis vines and surrounded by peonies, irises, foxgloves and bell flowers in early summer. When they finish blooming, rose bushes become a green backdrop for the flowers of late summer and fall.

Alba roses are the perfect starter rose for the disbeliever. The alba roses, which are cold hardy to USDA Hardiness Zone 3 or 4, and heat tolerant to Zone 8, are the most rugged, shade-tolerant and disease-resistant antiques. They make attractive upright shrubs, densely covered with bluish green leaves. These shrubs typically grow from 4 to 6 ft. tall, making them suitable for the back of the border.

Rosa 'Felicite Parmentier' is a compact shrub that quickly attains a height of about 4 ft. and is nearly as broad. Its unusual fat, round, creamy yellow buds open to full, flesh pink flowers that exude a sweet perfume. The blossoms are so packed with petals that they curve, or "reflex," backward and appear quartered. A bushy shrub of similar size is the aristocratic *R.* 'Konigin von Danemark' ('Queen of Denmark'). This lovely sovereign blankets herself with large buds of dark pink that open to full, scented, pale pink flowers that are quartered with a buttonlike center, or "eye." Both of these roses look particularly fine when faced with big, loose, blue-flowered ornamental herbs such as catmint (*Nepeta* ;x *faassenii* 'Dropmore' and *N. sibirica* 'Souvenir d'André Chaudron').

R. 'Céleste' is one of our favorite alba roses in the Morris Arboretum cottage garden. Its characteristic bluish foliage provides a lovely backdrop for its soft pink flowers. Three bushes spaced a foot apart will quickly create a sturdy shrub about 5 ft. high and less broad. Its masses of small, flesh pink flowers are effective with tall foxgloves (*Digitalis purpurea*), huge mauve globes of star of Persia (*Allium cristophii*) and purple spikes of flowering sage (*Salvia* × *superba*).

> *"When they finish blooming, rose bushes become a green backdrop for the flowers of late summer and fall."*

DAMASKS ARE THE BEST REPEAT-BLOOMING ANTIQUES

Many popular roses bloom in June and then bloom again after a brief pause. Some bloom until frost, seeming to flower continuously. To encourage repeat bloom, prune roses hard in spring and remove spent flowers after each bloom period.

Damask roses (Zones 5 to 8) are the hardiest and most disease resistant of these antique roses. They contribute fragrance, vigor and a long

The small, clustered pink flowers of the polyantha rose 'The Fairy' appear from summer through fall, making it a fitting companion for daylilies.

White-spired flowers of butterfly bush and soft-textured leaves of lamb's ears tone down the hot-pink roses of 'China Doll'.

A reblooming rose produces a crop of flowers in spring and autumn. The double, fuchsia-red flowers of 'Rose de Rescht' are framed by blue 'Six Hills Giant' catmint.

Blue 'Super Ego' Siberian iris and airy white *Crambe cordifolia* flowers complement the double pink blooms of 'Gertrude Jekyll' roses.

flowering season to the mixed border. A compact, tidy habit makes them well suited to small gardens. These are the workhorses of the repeat-blooming antique group. If you have space in your garden for only a few rose bushes, choose from among these unpretentious champs.

R. 'Rose de Rescht' is one of the best and most compact of the damasks. Its flowers are fuchsia-red and scented, with packed petals that fade to purple as they age. Flowers are produced freely in late spring with liberal autumn repeat blooming.

'Rose de Rescht' is best displayed in a mass or drift of several plants, blended with soft blue and lavender flowers and burgundy and silver foliage. To create a stunning combination, plant lavender-flowered fountain butterfly bush (*Buddleia alternifolia*) and purple-leaved smokebush (*Cotinus coggygria* 'Velvet Cloak') as a background. Then underplant 'Rose de Rescht' with blue sprays of catmint.

In the cottage garden here at the Morris Arboretum, a group of three 'Rose de Rescht' bushes forms part of a layered composition positioned in front of *R. glauca* (Zones 2 to 7), one of the few roses prized for its foliage. Its leaves are bluish gray with a distinct burgundy cast. Starlike single flowers in June are eventually followed by prominent red hips (fruit). The silvery, lacy leaves of artemisia envelope 'Rose de Rescht', and to complement its fuchsia-colored June flowering, we add the huge lavender flower globes of star of Persia faced with spikes of *Salvia* × *superba* 'Blue Hill' and a skirt of magenta-flowered cranesbill (*Geranium sanguineum* 'Alpenglow').

The best known of the damasks, 'Marchesa Boccella', is rarely out of bloom from June to hard frost. It is a bushy, 3- to 4-ft.-tall shrub, crowned with tight clusters of fat crimson buds that open to very double, fragrant silver-pink flowers on short, bristly stems.

Underplant this rose with large, round-leaved, big betony (*Stachys macrantha*). Its satiny pink flowers look like fine gems when underplanted with a pillow of lamb's ears, such as *S. byzantina* 'Silver Carpet' or 'Big Ears'.

Damask roses will be eager to repeat their bloom if they are given a generous topdressing of compost in spring and an application of organic fertilizer in spring and again after flowering in early summer. In our garden, the foliage turns bronze by late summer from leaf problems, but it is not unattractive.

The compact bourbon rose *R.* 'Souvenir de la Malmaison' (Zones 6 to 9) is one of the best reblooming roses for a small garden, and the most reliable bourbon rose for both continuous bloom and disease resistance. This admired

rose should fill a position in the front of the border because it rarely exceeds 2 ft. in height. It freely offers its blush-pink, fragrant, many-petaled flowers from June until hard frost.

Here in the cottage garden, we use drifts of 'Souvenir de la Malmaison' as part of an everblooming exhibit that always attracts visitors. This rose fills the foreground in front of a mass of tall hybrid tea *R.* 'Dainty Bess', which has single, pink flowers with showy maroon stamens. A companion under-planting of lamb's ears looks handsome all season. And the small purple globes of the autumn-blooming *Allium thunbergii* tucked in behind the lamb's ears make a wonderful fall combination with the flesh pink flowers of 'Souvenir de la Malmaison'.

Spiky flowers are a pleasing contrast for roses. The yellow flowers of 'Graham Thomas', a modern shrub rose, are framed by the yellow and orange spikes of red hot pokers (*Kniphofia* cvs.).

Flowering spires of foxgloves add an upright accent to this planting.

Mounds of pink-flowering shrub roses fill the middle ground.

Spreading clumps of cranesbill cover the roses' bare ankles.

MODERN EVERBLOOMING SHRUBS ARE WORKHORSES

Polyantha, or sweetheart, roses (Zones 5 to 9) are lovely, compact, disease-resistant, ever-blooming shrubs covered with large clusters of small pompom-shaped flowers. We use drifts of sweetheart roses to create spots of all-season color in the foreground of mixed borders. When planted in groups of three to five, these roses behave like a drift of perennials. Prune polyanthas hard in spring, and shear after each bloom period. Fertilize in spring and again after the June flowering. Top-dress with compost annually.

Groups of polyantha roses mingle easily with drifts of perennials such as lamb's ears, cranesbill geraniums, pinks (*Dianthus* spp.) and lady's mantle (*Alchemilla mollis*). Two new, long-blooming blue perennials with contrasting shapes complete the picture: 'Blue Hill' salvia, with its blue flower spikes, and the mound-forming *Scabiosa columbaria* 'Butterfly Blue'.

'The Fairy' is one of the best-known and easiest to find of the polyantha roses. It can be used as a ground cover or specimen, and it is easy to integrate into perennial borders. It is a workhorse that blooms nonstop from late June to hard frost.

For its vibrant pink blooms, we use *R.* 'China Doll', which covers itself in huge clusters of lightly scented flowers. It makes a fabulous perennial drift of all-season color, underplanted with spring-blooming blue pansies, backed by summer-blooming 'White Profusion' butterfly bush (*Buddleia davidii* 'White Profusion') and mingled with drifts of the white-flowered Japanese anemone (*Anemone* × *hybrida* 'Honorine Jobert'), which blooms in autumn.

A few modern floribunda roses are tough, disease resistant shrubs well suited to the mixed border. *R.* 'Betty Prior' (Zones 5 to 9) is a charming, old-fashioned floribunda. Flowers are single, carmine-pink, slightly fragrant, and produced in clusters. Rarely out of bloom, shrubs grow about 4 ft. high and less wide. It is particularly attractive displayed with *Verbena bonariensis* and *Artemisia* 'Huntington'. It's a knockout all season.

The adventurous gardener will find much to enjoy and appreciate about both antique and modern shrub roses. These roses mingle easily with perennial companions in mixed borders, offering their blooms freely and asking little from the gardener in return. And repeat-blooming types can always be counted on to provide a spot of welcome color in the autumn border.

"We use drifts of polyantha roses to create spots of all-season color in the foreground of mixed borders."

Rarely out of bloom, 'Betty Prior' is beautiful all summer when combined with long-lasting plants such as the silvery 'Huntington' artemisia and purple sprays of *Verbena bonariensis*, shown here.

SPECIAL
TECHNIQUES

3

BEFORE YOU SINK A SHOVEL in the ground, take a moment to consider what your beds and borders need to be successful—that is, beyond beautiful plants. In this section, some of the country's top perennial gardeners will share some of their techniques for creating and maintaining beautiful beds and borders.

You'll learn some tried-and-true methods for laying out bed lines and preparing the soil in your beds. Perhaps you're on a budget or would like to grow plant varieties not available in local nurseries. If so, you'll discover how to propagate many of your own plants from seed. A noted horticulturist will teach you how to prune your perennials in mid-season to prolong bloom, delay bloom, or get a second flush of flowers. And you'll learn what to do if your beds begin to look tired or out of control after a few years.

BARBARA BLOSSOM ASHMUN

is a garden designer, the author of several books, including *Garden Retreats* and *The Garden Design Primer*, and a contributing editor for *Fine Gardening*.

Build a Bed *without* Breaking *Your Back*

Instead of digging down, build a compost pile on top of the site for a new bed. Simply rake the raw materials into a mound and let them compost for a season or two.

I'VE BUILT NEW BEDS two different ways: the hard way and the easy way. When I did things the hard way, I'd slice the existing sod with an edger, dig up the strips with a spade, and stack them upside down to compost. Then, I'd dig about a foot down into the new bed, turn the soil over, break it into small chunks, add finished compost, turn it again, and mix compost and soil to make a uniform blend. Finally, I'd rake it all smooth and level, admiring the fine, crumbly texture. This was good exercise and satisfying work.

When I moved to a larger lot encompassing two-thirds of an acre, the very idea of improving so much dense, clay soil seemed overwhelming. I tried numerous bed-building experiments, but no matter how much tilling or amending I did, it was never enough. Hand-digging might have worked, but the Herculean effort required to spade my large garden from end to end made the task simply unimaginable.

(ABOVE) Select a site and mark it. Author Barbara Ashmun uses a hose to outline the contours of a new bed.

(ABOVE RIGHT) Define the line between grass and bed by using an edger to create a shallow trench.

So I began searching for easier ways to build new beds. Finally, I've found one. It doesn't require much digging, I don't have to strip off the turf, and it costs almost nothing. In essence, I build a compost pile and let it ripen into a rich, organic bed that my plants just love. The process does take a little time, but if gardening has taught me anything, it's the joy of participating in the miracle of transformation. Turning seeds into flowers or leaves into soil makes me feel almost like an alchemist.

Now I build new beds whenever the inspiration strikes, but there's no question that fall is the ideal time to tackle the task. Autumn days are usually mild enough to make vigorous activity enjoyable. Materials for composting are plentiful: fallen leaves, spent flower foliage, and lawn clippings are everywhere. Perhaps best of all, in my mild climate, the compost cooks all winter, and by spring, when I'm anxious to get back into the garden, the bed is ready.

DON'T BOTHER TO TEAR UP THE LAWN

I first learned there was a better, or at least an easier, bed-building technique in *The Ruth Stout No-Work Garden Book*. I'd also heard about it from friends. They all said the easy way to create good soil is to simply compost right on the site of your future bed. After putting the technique to the test several times, I've learned that it works. And along the way, I've added a few refinements of my own to make the process even easier.

The first step is defining the area that you're going to turn into a bed. I use a garden hose to outline the area. I usually warm up the hose in the sun so it's soft and easy to work with. Heat makes it pliable enough to coax into whatever shape I've envisioned.

Once I decide on the shape and placement of the new bed, I use an edger and a shovel to dig a 6-in.-deep trench between the bed and the lawn. The trench keeps the edge crisp and stops the lawn from invading the bed.

Not that I worry too much about the lawn. In fact, I don't even bother to tear up the grass. Some folks spread newspaper, or even cardboard, on the turf to smother it. I've done that but find it unnecessary—the 3-ft.-high piles of organic material I heap on the site kill the grass just as effectively. Once the new bed is planted with shrubs, perennials, or annuals, the roots of the new plants don't seem to have any problem growing through a layer of what was once turf.

PILE THE BED HIGH FOR THE BEST RESULTS

The key to the easy bed-building method is building a pile that is at least 3 ft. high, so you need to have plenty of materials to compost. I heap on layers of grass clippings, leaves, spent rabbit litter, sawdust, vegetable peelings, half-finished compost from my bins, and old potting soil from last year's annual containers.

To get a hefty pile, you might think about networking with people in your neighborhood who are throwing out materials that would fuel a good compost pile. I've trained my

Load up with organic materials. Fallen leaves, grass clippings, and sawdust are just some of the ingredients the author uses for on-site composting in a new bed.

(LEFT) Pile the bed high. Wheelbarrow loads of almost anything organic are added to make the new bed's compost pile 3 to 4 ft. high.

(FAR LEFT) For a finishing touch, use a spade to clean and neaten the border and keep the lawn out of the planting area.

Selecting a Site That Works

I think of my garden as a laboratory, a place to experiment with color, texture, and fragrance. It's already full of colorful beds where I arrange perennials and flowering shrubs into pleasing compositions. But I'm still experimenting, and before I embark on a new venture, I've got to prepare a new workshop.

Before looking for a new spot, I consider the needs of the plants I want to use. If I'm planning a home for shade-loving astilbes and hydrangeas, for example, I'll need to find bed space beneath the canopy of deciduous trees or on the north side of the house.

Once I know my plants will be happy, I stroll around the yard, looking at potential places from different angles. Sometimes I sit on a garden bench or plop down on the lawn to study the scene. I might check out the views from inside the house, too. At this stage, I'm just playing with geometry, looking for a likely place to plunk down a new square, rectangle, circle, or oval bed.

This is also a good time to think about the eventual size of the future site's plants. When full grown, will they block a view or create one? If the new site is in front of a homely fence or shed, filling the bed with tall flowering shrubs and towering perennials will create a colorful screen.

Once I do get an idea for a bed, I use a garden hose (or two, if I'm thinking big) to outline the shape I've envisioned. I aim for gracefully contoured beds that are in proportion with nearby planting areas. I think repeating shapes and sizes adds order and unity to larger designs.

One of the most common mistakes people make when preparing a new bed is skimping on its size. So, if you're wondering how big to make a new bed, remember that too big is almost always better than too small.

neighbors to bring me tarp-loads of leaves after they've raked, and wheelbarrows of grass clippings after they've mown. Landscapers who work in the neighborhood are glad to deliver pickup loads of grass clippings—they save a dump fee. They drop them onto a gigantic tarp that I lay out in the driveway, and I wheelbarrow the clippings to the new bed site. I also collect sawdust from a nearby woodworking shop, and straw bedding and manure from friends who have rabbits, chickens, or other animals. Loading the wheelbarrow with my bounty and maneuvering it back and forth from driveway to bed entails a fair amount of work, but to me it's easier than digging.

Once the pile is in place, I finish it off by raking the materials into a soft, rounded mound. Then I sometimes even collect extra earthworms that wriggle out of the ground and onto the sidewalk after a rainstorm. I take them to the new bed site to help break down all the raw ingredients. "Get to work!" I tell the worms, and then dream of them busily burrowing, making rich, black soil while I relax and wait for spring to arrive.

If you live where it's cold, and winter puts the local landscape into a deep freeze, a new bed prepared in fall may not be ready by spring. You could speed the process along by adding an accelerant to the pile. (You can find accelerants for compost-making at most hardware stores or garden centers.) Another option would be draping a sheet of black plastic over the pile to absorb sunlight and keep it warm. Some gardeners say white or clear plastic works just as well. Be sure to punch holes into the plastic so water and air can get into the pile.

In the meantime, you'll have to cope with one of the easy method's biggest drawbacks: it's ugly. You'll have to spend several months looking at an oversized heap of decomposing stuff that looks like a pile of dirt.

*"When I've finished building the pile, I relax
and let nature take its course."*

LET NATURE FINISH THE JOB

When I've finished building the pile, I relax
and let nature take its course. Insects and
microorganisms will dine on this fabulous
feast and transform it into crumbly soil over
the next six months.

If I'm in a big hurry, I turn the pile often
and keep it damp. If I'm in a bigger hurry, I
buy finished compost, pile it up 3 ft. high in
the shape of the bed, and plant. I did that one
fall, and thought I would be struck by light-
ning for sheer decadence, but instead I enjoyed
a beautiful island bed of Siberian irises and
daylilies the following spring.

Would I go back to the hard way of bed-
building? I figure I have three choices: I can
spend energy to hand-dig and amend soil,
spend money to buy finished compost to pile
on, or spend time waiting for raw materials to
break down. At this point, I like the last
option best. I'm willing to wait. There's plenty
of gardening to do in other borders while the
compost cooks. And it's fun to participate in a
natural process, creating a small ecosystem
where the slow process of decomposition gets
an assist from soft rains, warm sunshine, and
wriggling worms. I love being a small part of a
much bigger scheme.

A pile planted with
daylilies and irises set-
tled into a handsome
bed within a few
seasons.

BARBARA ALLEN

is a garden designer in Atlanta. She is an active member of the Georgia Perennial Plant Association and teaches classes on garden design and gardening with perennials.

Drawing the Line on Curved Beds & Borders

These sweeping beds lead to the front entry, illustrating how beds and borders can be used to direct eye flow and highlight focal points in the yard.

DESIGNING PLANTING BEDS for flat lots with symmetrical houses is easy. I simply work from a geometric plan, perhaps creating a parterre for a formal house. But here in north Georgia, I rarely encounter flat property. Our sloping lots call for curved, free-form beds, even when houses are symmetrical and traditional, with a door in the middle and two windows on each side.

Of course, there are other reasons to create sweeping beds and borders. Lower maintenance is one, especially on slopes that are difficult to mow. Here, I prefer island beds with trees, shrubs, and easy-care perennials.

Large beds that flow loosely from one side of a yard to the other can make your property appear larger. By keeping plantings in curving beds, grass forms a flowing river around them, making the garden appear more orderly. A well-maintained edge also lends a neat, cared-for look to the yard, even when the lawn needs to be mowed.

On slopes, island beds make a good alternative to grass That way, there's less to mow.

And finally, keeping the trees and plants in island beds provides a nice contrast in color—the soft brown of the mulch against the green of grass. Even in winter, when the warm-season grasses turn the color of hay, the soft brown of fallen leaves and pine straw creates a beautiful textural composition.

WORK WITH THE LAND, DON'T FIGHT IT

When laying out an island bed, one of the first things I do is look up. Beds should extend beyond the drip line of trees so that leaves or needles will fall into the bed instead of in the lawn.

Leaving the needles or leaves in place also provides a natural mulch that supplies all the nutrition that most trees and shrubs need. The mulch keeps roots cool, preserves moisture during hot summers, and prevents weed seeds from germinating. Also, trees are much safer here than in the lawn where their bark is subject to lawn-mower damage.

When possible, existing shrubbery should also be contained within beds and borders, as should natural features like rock outcrops or boulders. On a recent project, I ran into a small rock outcrop hiding under some ivy near a bed, so I removed the ivy and moved the bed line to include the stones.

It's important to take cues from the natural contours of the land—following the rises and falls in your property. Recently, I was working in a backyard that sloped from the deck to a creek. I established sweeping paths that criss-crossed the property twice, making a gentle walk to the creek. Curving island beds were planted between the paths.

In front yards, I make the home's entry the focal point, with beds and borders directing the eye to the door. I also like to make beds that flow from one side of the property to the other—arching across the lawn in strong, sweeping curves and deep dips. Sidewalks and driveways may become part of the design, or I

Include sidewalks in curved garden beds by crossing them at a near-90-degree angle.

may cross over them at near-90-degree angles, continuing the beds on the other side.

For a new house where the land has been scraped bare, I create beds for new trees to provide privacy and to screen unwanted views. On the south and west sides of the house, I plant deciduous trees for shelter from the summer sun; in winter, when their leaves drop to the ground, the sun can warm the house. On the north side, I plant evergreens to protect the house from winter winds.

LAY IT OUT WITH A HOSE

The easiest way to lay out a curved bed or border is with a garden hose or soft rope. I prefer a hose because it tends to curve naturally, even when stretched out. Sometimes I let the way the hose falls determine whether the bed will curve in or out. At this stage, it's important to loosen up and experiment. I make adjustments by kicking the hose around, creating broader curves and deeper dips, until the shapes of the beds and grass look like giant puzzle pieces.

With the aid of a garden hose, Barbara Allen lays out a new border. The hose can be easily moved to experiment with different shapes and curves.

Often, I create beds with lines that remind me of the divided continents on a map.

Once the beds are roughly laid out, I walk across the street to see how they look. If the borders can be seen from the house, I also check the window views from inside. I want to make sure the beds look good from all angles. Once I am satisfied, I mark the edges with blue landscape paint, which can be sprayed with the can in an upside-down position. I prefer blue paint because it is noticeable, but not glaring, in case the lines must be adjusted. (Instead of landscape paint, lime can be sprinkled on the ground or the hose can be left in place.) It's always good to live with these out-

Curved beds need a manicured
edge. The author recommends
digging a small trench around
the edge to keep out weeds;
edging materials would detract
from the natural appearance.

Bed line extends to the tree's dripline so leaves can mulch the ground where they fall.

Deep dips help define the curve of the bed, while soft curves are hardly noticeable.

Trenching is more pleasing to the eye than edging in an informal garden.

lines for awhile, adjusting them as leaves fall or adapting them to the changing patterns of sun and shadow.

KEEP EDGING UNOBTRUSIVE

Once the final changes have been made, I trench the edges. Visually, edging should not be more important than the garden. Unlike geometric beds, where I would use edging materials to call attention to the design and formality, I rarely use permanent edging on curved beds. They are distracting, causing your eyes to focus on the lines instead of the plants within the beds. Also, as the trees and shrubs grow, bed lines may need to be altered.

My favorite way to edge a bed is with a smaller version of the English ha-ha—a deep, narrow trench used to keep sheep out of the garden. It can be seen only up close. From afar, it goes almost unnoticed. My miniature version is 6 in. wide and 6 in. deep, giving my beds an adequate and unobtrusive buffer from encroaching weeds and grass. The mini-ha-ha is easy to maintain. Two or three times a year, I simply walk around the beds, touching up any rough spots with a garden hoe. With my bed lines established and edged, I'm ready to remove or kill the grass, amend the soil, and fill the island beds with my favorite flowering shrubs and perennials.

TRACY DiSABATO-AUST

has been lecturing on
perennials for 20 years.
She is the author of *The
Well-Tended Perennial
Garden: Planting and
Pruning Techniques.*

Pruning
Perennials in
Midseason

By selectively pruning
perennials in mid-
season, the author
achieves shaplier
plants, staggered or
prolonged bloom
times, and fresh foliage
growth.

THE FIRST TIME I cut back a drift of asters
in the middle of their summer growth spurt,
I felt both excited and anxious. Would my
pruning help or hinder the growth of these
perennials? Would they still bloom profusely? My experiment resulted in sturdier-stemmed plants
that didn't fall over when besieged by late-summer rains.
And their bloom spell, though delayed, proved as prolific
as ever. Soon I became hooked on midseason pruning of
perennials to achieve specific effects.

Through trial-and-error, I discovered ways to grow fuller,
more compact plants, to create interesting layering of
plants or plantings, and to stagger or delay bloom times. In
general, I have found that perennials are very forgiving, as
long as they are not unduly stressed.

It's not just tall-growing asters that look better with a
little judicious pruning before they flower. Many other
summer- and autumn-flowering perennials can be

1. Pinching removes an inch or less of the growing tip. Fingers are the tool of choice for this pruning method.

2. Use hand pruners to cut back individual stems. The author prunes a planting of willow-leaved sunflowers.

3. Shearing takes less time. Use hand shears to cut back large areas quickly. New growth soon covers stubbles.

"Pruning before flowering usually produces fuller plants with more bushy, branching stems."

trimmed to reduce their height, thus avoiding the need for staking (sidebar, pp. 114–115). And I would much rather prune than stake.

In areas with high winds, it may be necessary to cut back certain perennials before they flower to prevent them from flopping. Overly rich soil, or too much shade for sun-loving plants, may also produce leggy growth. Pruning before flowering usually produces fuller plants with more bushy, branching stems. However, with some species, such as cardinal flower (*Lobelia cardinalis*), flowers will be smaller, but more numerous. I often prefer these more modest blooms for cut-flower arrangements.

LAYER TO PROMOTE GRACEFUL SHAPES

Pruning plants before they flower can also be used to create interesting height gradations. As they mature, some perennials, such as bee balm (*Monarda didyma*), lose many leaves on the bottom half of their stems. These "ugly legs" can detract from the overall appeal of the plant. By cutting the plant's outer stems lower than its inner stems, new lateral growth will emerge, making the plant appear fuller. These pruned plants will bear flowers lower on their outer stems. In a similar manner, a mass planting can be layered by cutting back the outer plants of the group, also resulting in greater fullness.

PRUNE TO DELAY OR STAGGER BLOOMS

Staggering or delaying the bloom times of perennials can be worthwhile to the gardener

for several reasons. Staggered bloom times can be achieved by pruning separate plants of the same species a week or so apart. This can extend the season of interest, especially in a mass planting, or in situations where a species is planted in several places in the garden. I will sometimes cut back parts of individual plants, leaving the rest unpruned. The plants will then flower gradually over a longer period, rather than flowering profusely for a short time. The bloom period for a plant can thus be extended by a few days to several weeks.

Pruning a plant or mass planting to delay flowering also can be used to coordinate the flowering of an early-blooming perennial with

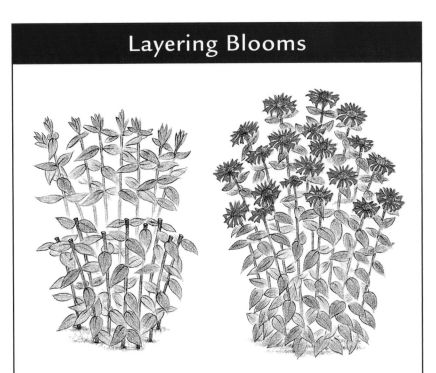

Layering Blooms

To layer a planting of perennials, cut back the outer stems as shown in the left illustration. With tall-growing plants, such as bee balm, new lateral growth will emerge, making the planting look fuller.

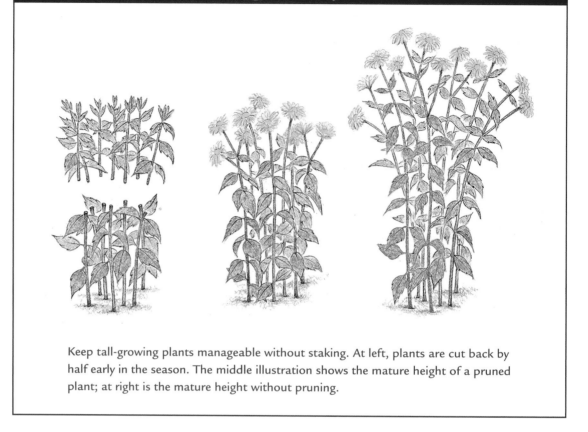

Promoting Sturdy Growth

Keep tall-growing plants manageable without staking. At left, plants are cut back by half early in the season. The middle illustration shows the mature height of a pruned plant; at right is the mature height without pruning.

a later-blooming species. This technique could also be used to benefit gardeners who want cut flowers of a certain species for longer in the season than usual. Gardeners who travel may opt to prune back their perennials in hopes of delaying blooms until they return from a trip.

PINCH, CUT BACK, OR SHEAR STEMS

The main techniques I use to prune perennials before flowering are pinching, shearing, and cutting back individual stems. The technique I choose depends on the perennial, my objectives and time constraints, and when I'm pruning.

To pinch a plant, remove only ½ to 1 in. of the growing tips. Fingers are the handiest tool for pinching. In warmer climates, to control the height of some perennials, such as asters,

it may be necessary to pinch stems two or three times during the growing season.

Cutting back a perennial may entail trimming 6 in. to 12 in. or more. Often I prune plants back by one-half or two-thirds of their height. I use bypass pruners or sharp pruning scissors to cut individual stems, usually above a lateral leaf.

Shearing cuts back many stems at once, and manual hedge shears are my tool of choice. While this method may leave some shaggy stubs of stems sticking up above leaves, plants will usually fill in quickly to hide the wounds.

Perennials with a bushy habit, such as chrysanthemums, respond better to shearing than perennials with a more open habit such as summer phlox (*Phlox paniculata*). One advantage of either cutting back or shearing over pinching is that it usually needs to be performed only once. In some cases, I combine techniques. For example, I may shear 'Lambrook Silver' artemisia (*Artemisia absinthium* 'Lambrook Silver') by a foot early in the season and then pinch it later to keep it shapely.

WHILE IT'S NOT EVERYTHING, TIMING MAKES A DIFFERENCE

I tend to concentrate most of my efforts on testing the effects of cutting plants back once before flowering. Although specific perennials can be cut back at different times—or several times—with different results, pruning many plants at one time is most efficient for a busy home gardener or landscape professional. I usually prune summer-flowering perennials by one-half or two-thirds in the first or second week of June. This is when I also cut back many spring-flowering species after they've bloomed, thus simplifying my garden maintenance.

In the Midwest, pruning in early- to mid-June delays the flowering of many summer-blooming perennials by as many as 7 to 20 days. Pruning earlier may be preferable if no delay is desired. To delay the flowering of autumn-blooming species, I prune them later in the season.

Gardeners in warmer climates may need to cut back perennials earlier in the season, and more severely, to effectively reduce their height. Also, with a longer growing season in these areas, autumn-flowering plants may be able to be pruned later to delay blooms. However, late pruning in cold climates may result in plants that don't have a chance to flower before frost.

In the Midwest, a common guideline is to prune late-blooming perennials by July 4 to ensure flowering before frost. This may be true with many perennials, but it's not set in stone. I have experimented with trimming certain perennials, such as asters, in late July or early August, and they still flowered before cold weather set in. Also, keep in mind that cutting back closer to the normal bloom time may create a greater delay in flowering. While cutting back early in the season may not delay blooms, it usually affects the plant's size.

Not all perennials respond well to pruning before flowering. Some may show a decrease in their floral display, the overall vigor of the plant, or both. Others may not flower at all. There are little scientific data about why perennials react differently to pruning. Keep in mind that this type of pruning is still experimental, which is part of the fascination it holds for me. I try to record many variables about my experiments in a notebook. Most important, I take time to observe and enjoy the results.

Staggering Bloom Times

Create staggered bloom times by cutting some plants back and leaving others unpruned. This extends the season of interest.

Success Stories from a Pruning Pioneer

Since pruning is species-specific and involves many variables, generalizing can be hazardous. Nonetheless, I will share some of my experiences with midseason pruning in my central Ohio garden. Your own techniques and timing will be influenced by your objectives and schedule, weather conditions, the age of the plant, and even soil conditions.

LAYERING SHASTA DAISIES HIDES BARE LEGS

'Alaska' Shasta daisy (*Leucanthemum* × *superbum* 'Alaska') normally grows 3 to 4 ft. tall. Unstaked, it often falls over in heavy summer rains. Unfortunately, this usually occurs just as the plants reach their peak bloom. To control their height, I pinched some plants one time in late May. They became fuller than unpruned plants, flowered at 18 to 20 in., and didn't require staking. Blooms of pruned plants were delayed by one week and there was no noticeable reduction in flower size. I have also pinched Shasta daisies to layer a planting and to hide the bare stems of taller unpruned daisies.

CUTTING BACK BALLOON FLOWERS PREVENTS FLOPPING

Balloon flower (*Platycodon grandiflorus*) tends to flop, so I was pleased that pruning it back by half in early June resulted in lush, compact plants 18 to 24 in. high, rather than 3 to 3½ ft. Blooms were delayed by 2 to 3 weeks.

EXTEND THE FLOWERING SEASON FOR PURPLE CONEFLOWER BLOOMS

I have several groupings of 'Bright Star' coneflower (*Echinacea purpurea* 'Bright Star') in my gardens. To extend their season of interest, I cut back some plants by one-half in early June when they were about 2½ ft. tall. They started to flower 2 to 3 weeks later than normal. Before I went on vacation in early July, I sheared another group of plants by about 1 ft. while they were about 3 ft. tall and in bud. The plants looked a bit shaggy after pruning, but they recovered nicely and flowered from mid-August until early October.

KEEP LANKY CONEFLOWERS STATELY WITHOUT STAKING

'Herbstsonne' coneflowers (*Rudbeckia nitida* 'Herbstsonne') can easily reach 7 ft. Although the stems of this tall perennial are reportedly self-supporting, they topple in my gardens without light support. To avoid staking, I cut them back by one-half in early June when they're 2 ft. tall. This produces 4½- to 5-ft.-tall, freestanding plants that flower about a week later than usual.

PRUNED HELIOPSIS FLOWERS LATER ON SHORTER STEMS

When grown in full sun, 'Sommersonne' heliopsis (*Heliopsis helianthoides* ssp. *scabra* 'Sommersonne') doesn't normally flop. But, sometimes I prune them to extend the bloom period or to layer a planting. I cut them back by one-half in early June. They flowered at 2½ to 3 ft., instead of their normal 5 ft. Flowering was delayed by about 10 days. There was no reduction in flower size.

The budding Shasta daisies in front were pinched in late May. Their foliage looked fuller, and the plants bloomed a week later than the unpruned daisies behind them.

SHEAR 'SNOWBANK' BOLTONIA FOR A FULLER, LAYERED LOOK

'Snowbank' boltonia (*Boltonia asteroides* 'Snowbank') usually doesn't require staking if it's grown in full sun and sheltered from winds. However, plants grown in more exposed areas or part shade do tend to fall over. 'Snowbank' boltonia can be pruned in several ways. If plants are cut back by half in early June, there's usually no delay in flowering but they grow more compact. One year, I sheared back the outer stems of certain plants in a large clump by about one-third in mid-July. The outer stems bloomed at 2½ ft. tall rather than 4 ft. tall and started flowering about a week later than the unpruned inner section. This created an interesting layered effect to the planting.

TRIMMED PHLOX YIELDS SMALLER BLOOMS

Summer phlox (*Phlox paniculata*) responds well to cutting back or pinching to reduce height or delay flowering. I've cut some plants back by one-half in early- to mid-June. With others, I trimmed 6 in. off the tips when the plants were in tight bud. There was usually a 2-week delay in flowering. If plants are cut back in May, expect less of a delay. Pruned plants produced smaller blooms, which I prefer for arrangements.

I also used pruning to rectify a jarring color combination. The cotton-candy pink flowers of *Phlox paniculata* 'Flamingo' looked awful with a yellow-orange daylily that I had planted it behind. The bad match became apparent when they flowered at the same time. I didn't want to move either of them, so the following year I pruned the phlox to delay its bloom time. I cut

it back by one-half in early June and shaped it by cutting the outer stems shorter than the inner ones. It flowered from top to bottom at 18 in., rather than its normal size of 2 ft. Most important, it bloomed 2 to 3 weeks later than normal, after the daylily blossoms were spent.

PRUNED SUNFLOWERS GROW FULLER

Willow-leaved sunflower (*Helianthus salicifolius*) normally reaches 5 to 6 ft. and is self-supporting. But if plants are grown in partial shade, stems will be weak and flop. Also, a shorter, fuller plant may sometimes be desirable. In these cases, plants can be pinched or cut back. Plants pinched in early July flowered at 3 ft. with no delay in their normal bloom time of late September.

These 'Bright Star' coneflowers were pruned by a foot in early July. The pruned plants flowered in mid-August, two weeks later than the others.

Phlox paniculata 'David' was cut back by half in mid-July when it was in tight bud to delay flowering. It bore smaller flowers in mid-August.

MARIETTA O'BYRNE

and her husband, Ernie, own Northwest Garden Nursery in Eugene, Oregon, which specializes in perennials. Marietta lectures and teaches on various areas of gardening.

Start *with* Seeds

for a Collector's Paradise

Plentiful plantings are part of the bounty of seeds. The relatively low cost of growing from seed makes using large drifts of plants, such as these primroses, an affordable goal.

I WAS 6 WHEN I DISCOVERED the magic of seeds. My gardening was limited to fiddling with a flower box on the balcony, but I'll never forget the day I watched a pansy burst open to spill its trove of tiny, brown seeds. There, right before my eyes, was a miracle, the start of new life. I still feel a thrill when I'm working with seeds, and so does my husband, Ernie. It's a good thing, because growing plants from seed has made all the difference to our garden.

We always wanted a big ocean of a garden, one swept by waves of color and awash in curiosities. As passionate plant collectors, we hungered for the unusual and the exotic. We yearned to experiment with plants from the far Himalayas or distant South America, plants we weren't even sure would grow in our USDA Hardiness Zone 7 garden.

But when we heard talk of "large drifts" and "exotic specimens," we saw dollar signs. On our budget, the garden we dreamed of would have been impossible. But we could

acquire and trade seeds. After all, seeds are cheap—you can usually buy a packet full of seeds for a lot less than you might pay for a single perennial. And, with a bit of research, seed raising is not difficult: With a container, a handful of soil, and a little patience, we grow almost any plant. We already had a nice garden, with trees, shrubs, and perennials purchased from garden centers, but seeds helped to bring the whole thing to life. We've used their magic to enhance our garden, with masses of primroses (*Primula* spp.), elegant drifts of wine-red poppies (*Papaver* spp.), and a host of botanical treasures.

We now expect to grow great plants from seeds, but there have been a few unanticipated rewards as well. We always loved Siberian iris (*Iris sibirica*), but voracious armies of slugs seemed to like them even more and usually ate at least half the buds. Then we obtained some seeds for an unnamed tetraploid Siberian. The word "tetraploid" always piques our interest

because it usually promises deeper colors, heavier textures, and larger flowers. The iris seeds took three years to flower, but they produced the most beautiful Siberians we have seen and, for some mysterious reason, slugs don't touch them. How can you beat that?

SELECT SEEDLINGS WITH VARIATIONS IN FLOWERS OR FOLIAGE

I've been sowing seeds every year since that day on the balcony. When we moved to a more rural area, I built a garden and planted it with marigolds, sweet peas, and lettuces. Later, as a wandering young adult, I grew peas in Ireland, lettuces in Greece, and geraniums on a houseboat in California. I eventually married a plant-loving man named Ernie and settled in Oregon, where I worked my way through every vegetable in the seed catalog. After our children grew up, Ernie and I really indulged our passion for plants. We've become dedicated collectors, especially of rock garden plants, and love to grow such oddities as *Calceolaria darwinii*, a petite charmer from the Andes that waves yellow and maroon house slipper–shaped flowers on a 3-in. mast, and *Jurinella moschus*, a diminutive plant from Iran with poofy, 1¼-in. pink pompoms.

Our tastes are eclectic. Besides rock garden plants, we collect anything and everything as long as it's pretty. We are especially fond of plants with purple or black foliage, and having lots of seedlings makes it possible for us to select those plants with the richest, darkest colors. All we have to do is keep an eye on the young plants as they grow. Each batch of seedlings yields a few offspring that are slightly different from their siblings. They may be taller or shorter than the rest, or the flower may be a slightly different color. We're always

on the lookout for those variations and collect seeds from the ones we like best.

We planted a lovely, plum-colored variety of the opium poppy (*Papaver somniferum*) that set seed with abandon. Every season, we kept only seeds of the darkest offspring. After a few generations, we had some almost black variations. Now they've self-sown in unexpected parts of our perennial beds, but plum and black are great colors that fit into almost any color scheme.

Then there's the plant I think of as the "Queen of Blacks," *Cimicifuga simplex* 'Brunette', commonly called snakeroot. It's one of the most sought-after plants in years.

Not long ago, a single plant went for $50, and they were hard to find even at that price. Ernie and I bought one plant and decided to try its seeds. Through experimenting, we found they need a double dormancy—that means they have to go through two winters in our garden before deigning to germinate. Temperatures of 40°F or below are usually adequate for seeds that need a stretch of cold weather to break dormancy. Once they do, we comb through the seedlings and use the pick of the litter to make luxurious, mass displays. We love overhearing people whisper, "They must have paid a fortune for those."

A riotous sweep of seed-grown plants anchors an abundant border. *Clematis recta* 'Purpurea', at lower left and center, contrasts with the coral blooms of *Alstroemeria* 'Ligtu Hybrids', at lower center.

An Unconventional Seed-Starting Strategy

We don't start seeds the way most gardeners do. Our seeds spend most of winter outside, and they don't get any bottom heat. Our method works well for just about everything we grow.

Most of our seeds—except for those of tender annuals and others that will be lethally affected by cold—go into pots in late January and early February. We usually start tender plants six to eight weeks before the frost-free date. Plants that grow best from fresh seed, like many *Ranunculus* species should be started as soon as they come off the plant. In fact, we sometimes buy a plant just to collect its seeds—doing this ensures us the seed is fresh.

We begin with a 4-in. pot filled with a mix of half perlite and half Black Gold, a peat- and compost-based product. Any soilless mix will do, as long as it's blended with an equal amount of perlite or vermiculite.

SCATTER SEEDS ON TOP OF THE SOIL, THEN ADD CHICKEN GRIT

Most gardening books suggest that you bury, or at least cover, seed, but we get excellent results by sowing thinly on top of the mix and pressing the seeds firmly into it. For large seeds, we press a little harder. Then the pot gets topped off with a ¼ in. of No. 2 chicken grit, which is available at any feed store. Aquarium gravel works too, as long as the stones are between ⅛ in. and ¼ in. in diameter. (Don't use limestone unless the plant likes alkaline soil.) This topping keeps the seeds separate and prevents them from being washed into a corner when we water. It also helps keep the soil moist.

Labeling each pot is next. Plants whose names we thought we'd remember in winter are forgotten by spring. A white, plastic label and a pencil are all it takes to record the variety, the date—including the year—of sowing, and the source of the seed. We also note any special conditions the plant may require—if it should be planted in a rock garden, for example.

PUT POTS OUTSIDE IN WINTER

Finally, we water gently, using a spray wand or by placing the pot in a saucer of water. We try to get a good feel for the weight of a well-watered pot; later, if one feels light, we know it's time to water. Pots go outside, under the eaves of a roof so they don't get too much rain. We keep them out of full sun or deep shade—eastern exposures provide ample light.

Tender annuals get a later sowing, but otherwise we use the same method, even though cool weather may start them off slowly. After seedlings emerge, they tend to be more frost sensitive. In case of unseasonal frost, protect them in a cold frame or with a light covering. Sometimes we don't start heat-loving plants such as morning glories until later in spring or early summer; the extra warmth encourages vigorous growth, and the young plants quickly make up for lost time. Plants with a late start can also be used to fill holes in the late summer border when earlier blooming flowers are starting to wane.

Then we wait—the seeds of some perennials and rock garden plants may not germinate for two or more years. But since there are so many seedlings coming up at any time of year, we don't really notice that some take longer than others. We keep the pots evenly moist, but if one doesn't show any sign of life by the third spring, we give up on it.

Perhaps because I grew up in Germany, where "frische luft" (fresh air) is considered a cultural concept and an essential tonic for children, I think it is also good for seedlings. We leave them outside instead of closed up in a greenhouse, and the extra air circulation they get outdoors seems to prevent problems with fungus or damping off.

TO TRANSPLANT, EMPTY OUT A POT OF SEEDLINGS

We let seedlings grow a bit before transplanting. Most references say seedlings can be transplanted as soon as they show their first pair of true leaves; we get better results by waiting.

When transplanting, we always work in a cool, shady place so the seedlings aren't stressed by heat or sunlight. Then, instead of pricking the seedlings out one by one, we gently turn out the whole pot on its side. The loose, soilless mix crumbles readily, so separating the seedlings is easy. Then, holding the seedlings only by their leaves, we pot them up in a mix that's half commercial potting soil and half washed sand or grit. We also add slow-release fertilizer. Most perennials and annuals go into 4-in. pots; rock garden and other tiny plants go into 2-in. pots.

Then we wait some more. Most perennials and annuals are planted as soon as they look strong enough to survive in the garden. Plants left too long in pots can get root bound and may never fully recover. The annuals soon put on a fine show; the perennials usually fill out within a couple of months, though they rarely bloom the first year.

Scatter seed thinly over the surface of a soilless mix, then press seeds into the mix.

A label and layer of chicken grit add the final touch to a pot of just planted seeds.

To transplant seedlings, gently empty a pot full of them. The soilless mix crumbles effortlessly and individual seedlings can be easily separated.

Hold young seedlings by their leaves only, and use a finger to poke a planting hole into a new pot.

Seedlings sometimes yield surprises. An iris the slugs won't touch grew from a batch of unnamed tetraploid iris seeds.

SEEKING NEW DISCOVERIES

We've discovered that some of the plants we find most desirable can be purchased only as seeds. Perhaps more important, both of us derive a real satisfaction in nurturing a plant that started life as a seed halfway around the world and making it feel at home in our garden. With plenty of seedlings, we can try unfamiliar plants in a variety of microclimates to increase the odds for success.

We have as much fun finding new plants to try as we do planting the seeds. Our favorite winter pastime is perusing the seed lists we get from the Hardy Plant Society of Great Britain and the North American Rock Garden Society. Every year, we pick at least a couple of totally unknown plants, just for the excitement of growing them. Two years ago, our best new find was an annual, *Cerinthe major* var. *purpurascens*, with bluish, white-spotted

❧

"When a seed is hard to start, look for clues in the plant's natural environment."

foliage and small, purple flowers enclosed in dark blue, leaflike bracts.

IF SEEDS DON'T SPROUT, LOOK FOR CLUES IN THEIR NATIVE ENVIRONMENT

Discovering unique varieties and intriguing plants is just part of the experimentation that is often crucial to success with seeds. The seeds of that dark-leaved snakeroot weren't the only ones we've had to tinker with over the years. The double dormancy they required isn't, in fact, all that unusual. We've since learned that the seeds of many plants must undergo specific conditions to break dormancy and germinate.

When a seed seems hard to start, clues can often be found in the plant's natural environment. We've learned a lot by consulting reference books that tell us how plants grow in the wild. Seeds of some woodland plants, such as *Jeffersonia*, *Corydalis*, and most of the *Ranunculus* species, have ephemeral seeds, which means they must be fresh to germinate. That makes sense when one considers that they live in an ever-moist environment, and, as soon as their seeds ripen in the wild, they drop on the damp ground into the decaying litter, so they never dry out. Fresh seed gave much better results. On the other hand, seeds from plants native to deserts or regions with dry summers are likely to rot if planted fresh.

Sometimes the process required for a seed to break dormancy is even more complex. On our recent plant-hunting excursion to South Africa, we learned that its grasslands are prone to fires. The seeds of many natives, such as some heaths (*Erica* spp.) and sedges (*Carex* spp.) will not sprout unless they have gone through a fire. Botanists at the Kirstenbosch Botanical Garden in Capetown found that it was smoke, not heat, that dissolved the chemi-

Unusual plants grown from seed add flair to the garden. The dark foliaged, creamy-flowered *Anthriscus sylvestris*, 'Ravenswing', at lower left, makes an alluring addition to a planting of *Alstroemeria* 'Ligtu Hybrids', *Delphinium* cultivars and the floribunda rose 'White Simplicity'.

cal inhibitors in the seed coat that prevented germination. Now the garden sells smoke-impregnated paper disks. Just place the disk in some water, soak your seeds, and plant.

MAKE YOUNG PLANTS AT HOME IN THE GARDEN

Once we get the seedlings into the ground, we face another challenge—finding good ways to use the exotic plants effectively. We keep a reference library and highly recommend investing in at least one plant encyclopedia that includes cultural information. This is also important when perusing seed lists composed solely of Latin names.

Using new plants together with old favorites can also be a challenge. Some of our best combinations have been almost acciden-tal. Discoveries even come while loading our truck with plants for a sale. I put a creamy-pink 'Little Showoff' daylily next to a *Salvia verticillata* 'Purple Rain' and liked the color combination so much that I plan to use it in our garden. There are other plant partnerships that came about serendipitously. Wandering around with a *Cerinthe major* var. *purpurascens*, I saw a manna grass (*Glyceria maxima* 'Variegata') that looked perfect as a backdrop.

Our seedlings generally prove healthier and longer-lived than purchased plants. They don't go through the trauma of shipping, storage, and climate changes, and they develop a better root system when planted young. Besides, we take well-earned pride in growing our own plants from seed.

Renovating
a Perennial Bed

CHRIS CURLESS

writes and edits the catalog for White Flower Farm. Always an avid gardener, Chris was previously an associate editor for *Fine Gardening*.

The first step in renovating a perennial bed is to empty it. A patch of lamb's-ears pops out of the soil on the blade of a spade.

FOR MOST GARDENERS, a perennial border is a work in progress. Every year we fine tune, shifting plants from one place to another and replacing plants that suddenly seem lackluster with others that have caught our fancy. But sometimes a border needs more than tinkering to make it right. It may need a whole new design. It may be under siege from tenacious weeds or perennials that aren't satisfied with their allotted space. Or it may require improved soil to reach its potential.

The solution in these cases is renovation, a new beginning for your border. You dig up all of the plants in the border—with a few exceptions—and prepare the soil, digging in organic matter, adjusting soil pH and adding fertilizer. You divide and reset the old plants you want to keep, and you add new ones. The result is a new border, one that has taken a giant step closer to being the border you want.

With all but a few of its plants removed, a perennial border looks as though it has been pounded by a hail of mortar shells. The bleeding-heart at the gardener's feet was left undisturbed, because it was covered with flower buds when this renovation was undertaken in late April.

Water from a wand moistens the perennials temporarily marooned on a plastic tarp. Uprooted plants can survive two days or more if protected from the sun and kept moist.

Renovating a perennial border is a big job, but it's within the reach of most gardeners. If your border is too large, or if you don't feel up to tackling the project, consider calling in a professional gardener. I used to work for a small perennials nursery in northwestern Connecticut. We put in a lot of new borders, but as much as half of our work was rehabilitating old ones. We tinkered when tinkering was required, but when a Band-Aid wasn't enough, we renovated. Although I garden for fun these days, I still have occasion to put my renovation skills to work.

The photos for this article were taken last April when I helped my friend and former assistant editor of *Fine Gardening* Renee Beaulieu overhaul the border in her front yard.

CLIMATE DETERMINES RENOVATION TIME

In most of North America, you can renovate in either spring or fall. The window of opportunity in spring opens as the soil thaws and dries out enough to be worked easily. By then most perennials have made enough growth that you can find them and identify them. The window closes as air and soil temperatures rise and plants grow too large to recover quickly from being moved or divided. In late summer or fall, the window opens as temperatures begin to cool, then closes at least a month before frost begins to creep into the soil.

The opening and closing dates of these windows vary widely from place to place and from year to year. Here in Connecticut, the best time for spring renovation is usually between mid-April and early May. The fall renovation season runs from late August to early October.

Geography may dictate the best time to renovate. Where winters are especially harsh—say, USDA Hardiness Zone 4 and colder—spring is the ideal time. Plants dug up and reset in spring are well established by winter, while plants disturbed in fall may not have time to become established before the arrival of cold weather. In areas where summers are hot and often dry and winters are relatively mild, fall or winter is the best time to renovate. Cooler temperatures and plentiful rainfall allow plants to settle in before the arrival of heat and drought the following spring.

For gardeners with a choice, both spring and fall have their advantages. Spring is the time when energy and enthusiasm for gardening are often at their peak; after a winter of sitting idle and salivating over plant catalogs, we are eager to get to work. By fall active gardeners are feeling a bit spent, but fall tends to be less hectic than spring, when every corner of the garden seems to require attention. You can also see the size and shape of the plants in the fall. In the spring, you're digging up plants that may be showing only a little top growth; you're working from your inevitably faulty memory as you try to reinvent your border.

PLAN BEFORE YOU DIG

Before you reach for your shovel, take some time to sketch out a new design if you're not happy with the existing one. Don't worry about neatness or whether your drawing is to scale. Your sketch is an attempt to solve a complicated puzzle—how to combine plants with varying heights, foliage textures, flower colors and bloom times into a pleasing whole. You aren't likely to produce a perfect plan as you pore over gardening books and catalogs in your armchair, but you do need to make some key decisions about the layout of your border-to-be in advance. The more decisions you make before you get to work, the faster and more smoothly the project will go.

Before you start digging, you should draw up a list of which plants will stay, which ones will go and which you must buy; your design will come in handy here. You'll also need to consider what to do with the plants you don't want or won't have room for in the renovated border. Look for other places in the yard that would benefit from the overflow. Or line up friends who are ready and willing to take bare-root plants off your hands.

In setting aside time for the renovation, consider the size of your border, the speed with which you work and whether you can count on help. A border 30 ft. or 40 ft. long and 8 ft. wide could require the efforts of two people for the better part of a weekend. Allow time for unanticipated complications. Like many other gardening jobs, renovation somehow takes longer than you expect.

GATHER TOOLS AND MATERIALS

Before you begin renovating a border, gather together the tools and supplies you'll need. You probably already own most of the digging tools. I use a spade to dig up plants. The blade cuts through plant roots, and the handle is short enough to allow me to pry even good-sized plants out of the ground without risk of breaking the tool. To loosen the soil and turn in amendments, I use a long-handled, round-point shovel. For planting, I use a trowel. A rigid steel rake smooths the bed before and after soil preparation, and a leaf rake comes in handy for cleaning the adjacent lawn of renovation debris—roots, soil amendments and mulch.

To divide plants that I can't pull apart with my hands, I use an old kitchen knife or a pruning saw (one I no longer use for pruning—soil quickly dulls saw teeth). The spade comes in handy for dividing large clumps.

In general, you'll need three sorts of supplies for renovation: soil amendments, fertilizers and mulch. No matter what kind of soil you have, you'll want to add organic matter, such as compost, manure or peat moss. Organic matter helps aerate clay soils and helps sandy soils hold more moisture. It's difficult to say how much organic matter you should add when preparing a bed. More is generally better; it's hard to overdo it. As a rule, I put down a layer about 2 in. or 3 in. deep and then turn it into the soil.

In addition to adding organic matter, you may need to add nutrients and adjust the pH of the soil. The only way to know what you need and how much you should apply is to test your soil.

Fertilizer speckles a layer of manure, compost and peat moss spread over the emptied border. Renovation provides a good opportunity to improve the soil.

Using a round-point shovel, a gardener turns amendments and fertilizers into the soil of her border.

Divide and multiply. One hardy geranium becomes two with the aid of an old kitchen knife. When renovating a perennial bed, divide plants to increase their numbers or to keep them vigorous.

Maybe a little more to the left. A hardy-geranium division joins other divisions and purchased plants in the new bed. Re-assembling a perennial border is like putting together a puzzle.

You'll probably want to mulch your newly planted bed, covering the soil with a material that both inhibits the germination of weed seeds and conserves moisture. Use an organic mulch, which improves the soil as it breaks down. Choose one that has a fine texture— 4-in. bark chips appear out of scale at the feet of daylilies and coreopsis. Appropriate mulches include shredded leaves and shredded or ground bark. Depending on where you live, you might also find packaged mulches, such as cocoa shells or buckwheat hulls, at nurseries and garden centers.

EMPTY THE BED

The first step in renovating a perennial border is to empty the bed of plants. Dig perennials by cutting a circle around the crown of the plant with a trowel or a spade and then prying the roots up. (The crown is the place where the roots meet the top growth.) For large perennials that haven't been disturbed in years, you may find it easier to cut the plants into manageable pieces with a spade or even an ax while they're still in the ground. Then lift out the smaller chunks one at a time.

You don't have to remove all the plants in the bed. In most cases, you should avoid disturbing shrubs, because they tend to be less forgiving of the rough treatment that perennials endure without much protest. You may also want to leave alone any perennials that are better divided at another time of year. If you grow peonies, for example, and you decide to renovate your border in spring, you should probably work around them. Odds are they would not flower well that year, even if you spare them the knife and just move them.

As you dig up the plants, set them on a plastic tarp spread out in a shady spot. If you don't know your plants by sight (and even if you do), keep them together in groups and label them; it's time-consuming to hunt among the heaps of roots, leaves and soil when you're ready to put the plants back in the bed. Water plants on the tarp occasionally (as weather conditions dictate) to keep them from drying out.

Most plants turn out to be much tougher than you might expect. If the weather is cool and the plants are kept in the shade and are well watered, they can survive out of the ground for two or three days, perhaps even longer, with no ill effects. You may lose a plant or two, but happily there are garden centers and mail-order catalogs full of plants ready to take their place.

PREPARE THE SOIL

With the plants out of the border, prepare the soil by digging in organic matter, other soil amendments (such as lime or sulphur) and fertilizer. Start by raking the soil even with a rigid steel rake. Then put down a layer of organic matter and sprinkle fertilizers over it. Beginning at one end, turn over the soil with a shovel or a fork, thoroughly mixing in the amendments and fertilizer. Work your way backward, away from those areas you've already dug, so you don't walk in the prepared soil. (One of the chief benefits of preparing soil is fluffing it up so that plant roots have ready access to oxygen; walking on soil compacts air spaces.) When you finish digging, rake the soil level again and clean spilled soil from the edge of the border so you can see where it ends and the lawn, path or edging material begins.

Many gardening books recommend double-digging perennial borders. Double-digging means loosening and amending the soil to a depth twice the length of a spade or shovel blade—between 18 in. and 24 in. I have no doubt that deeper is better, particularly in heavy clay soils, but by all accounts double-digging is very hard work. I've always had good results turning soil just one spade's depth. Choose the technique that is best for your plants and your body.

DIVIDE AND PLANT

Once the soil is prepared, replant the bed with old favorites and new additions. You could replant your border without dividing any of the perennials you dug up, but this is a good opportunity for dividing plants. Chances are you'll want more of some plants, and you'll want to divide others to keep them growing vigorously.

Dividing perennials is like performing an operation—with one important difference: plants don't have feelings, so there's no need for anesthesia. You just tug, cut or chop away, and from one clump you suddenly have 2, 3 or 12 plant pieces that, with a little care, soon recover and thrive on their own. If you are doing the work in fall, begin by cutting back the top growth to just a few inches in height. Then clean the soil from the roots by shaking the plant vigorously, dropping it on the ground or washing the roots off with water—whatever it takes to allow you to get a better view of the roots and the crown.

Different perennials require different dividing tools and techniques. You can often pull ground-covering plants, such as lamb's-ears or bee balm, apart with your bare hands. For small clump-formers you'll need a knife to separate stems. For larger plants you may need to jump up and down on a spade. If a plant has a woody center (ornamental grasses and astilbes are examples), a pruning saw or an ax comes in handy.

After you've finished dividing, set out the divisions and the newly purchased plants on the prepared soil of the border, arranging them to your taste. Don't do any planting until all of the plants are in place and you are satisfied

Put plants back in the ground. A trowel is used to dig a hole for a Siberian iris. Planting goes quickly in the fluffy soil of a newly prepared bed.

Create a natural blanket. A mulch of shredded leaves added after planting inhibits weed-seed germination and slows the evaporation of soil moisture.

"Don't be surprised if you find the need to deviate from your design."

⟋⟍

with the flow of the groupings and their spacing. (If the sun is shining, you need to make decisions quickly to keep bare-root plants from drying out.) Leave room for maintenance paths, which allow you access to perennials (and weeds) you can't reach from the edge of the border; you want to avoid stepping into the bed and compacting the soil as much as possible. If you want to include annuals in your border, remember to allow space for them, too.

Don't be surprised if you find the need to deviate from your design. Few people can sit down in front of a piece of paper and draw up a border that fits the site perfectly. You're bound to find that a tree at the back of the border casts more shade than you remembered. And you'll no doubt guess wrong about the number of plants you need to fill a spot. Be prepared to adapt your design to reality—and allow yourself to take advantage of inspiration as you stand in front of your new border, a division clutched in each hand.

When you're pleased with the arrangement, begin planting. The task of planting 50 perennials (the number that might fit in the border shown in the photographs that accompany this chapter) appears daunting, but it goes quickly if you turn it into a mechanical

process. Take a deep breath, grab a trowel and dig speedily. Pause to set the plant in the hole so the crown is even with the soil level of the bed, firm the soil around it and move to the next plant. If you are adding container-grown plants to your border, take a moment to break up the root ball a bit and tease the roots apart so that they will grow out into the soil. If a plant is badly pot-bound, make at least four vertical cuts in the sides of the root ball with a knife before planting it into the border.

MULCH AND WATER

You're almost finished. Mulch the new border with a 2-in. to 3-in. layer of organic mulch. Then water the plants thoroughly—even if rain is impending. I like to give the plants their first soaking by hand with a watering wand (not a spray gun), drenching every plant two or three times as I walk up and down the border.

Before you can call the job done, you have to clean up the debris and find homes for the plants still sitting on the tarp. Use a leaf rake or a broom to sweep up roots, stems and spilled mulch. Pick up pots and plant labels. Plant the extra plants and leftover divisions you want elsewhere in the garden; package up the rest in flats or in plastic bags for friends. Drag the remaining plants, along with the extra soil on the tarp, to the compost pile.

WATER DEEPLY

The only thing your border will require immediately after renovation is water. Water is particularly important for perennials disturbed in the spring. On a warm, windy spring day they lose more moisture through their leaves than they take up through their mangled roots. Some wilting is inevitable, even if the soil is moist. But if the soil dries out, you risk killing your plants or subjecting them to stress, making them more vulnerable to pests and diseases.

A gentle shower from a watering wand soaks a newly planted perennial border. Moisture—from the sky or a hose—is crucial to help perennials recover from the trauma of being divided and transplanted.

The renovated border, three months later, handsomely rewards the gardener's soil.

Watering is usually less critical in autumn, when plants are entering a period of dormancy. And in most parts of the country, autumn rains are plentiful enough to keep the soil constantly moist. But if rain doesn't fall, you should check the moisture of your soil regularly with your fingers, then water thoroughly as needed.

If you have rodents on your property or in your neighborhood, you may find signs of digging in your new border. Raccoons, skunks and squirrels love the scent of freshly turned soil. They aren't interested in your plants; they're after grubs and worms, or that nut they half-remember having buried in your garden. The damage they cause is usually aesthetic (your beautifully mulched bed can take on a pock-marked appearance overnight), but a hungry raccoon can sometimes toss a small division over his shoulder in his mad search for creepy-crawlies in the soil. Typically, patience wins out. After a week or two of tidying mulch and replanting exhumed plants, you should see the digging abate as the soil settles and rain washes away the smell of fresh earth.

Gardeners in cold-winter climates should apply a winter mulch—a 3-in. to 6-in. blanket of hay, straw or evergreen boughs—to a border renovated in fall. The purpose of a winter mulch is not to prevent frost from penetrating the soil, but instead to keep the soil frozen. On sunny days in late winter and early spring, the top few inches of soil may thaw out, only to refreeze quickly at night. The sudden expansion of the soil as it freezes can pop a perennial that is not well established right out of the ground—a process called heaving. Heaving exposes the roots to drying winds and killing cold. Apply a winter mulch after the ground has frozen in late fall. Remove the mulch in spring when temperatures below the freezing mark become infrequent.

Renovating a perennial border is a big project, but the improvement in the border's appearance and in the growing conditions for the plants more than repays the effort. You'll still find the urge to tinker after the job is done (after all, what would gardening be without tinkering?) but your new and improved border will be a quantum leap closer to the garden of your dreams.

GARDEN
GALLERY

4

THE ULTIMATE GOAL of many gardeners is a border that flowers all summer and looks good year-round. And while even the best-planned borders have seasons in which they shine the brightest, it is possible to create a border that is attractive in four seasons. One of our contributors will show you how.

Sunny, flat, open spaces with good, rich soil sound like the perfect setting for a mixed bed or border. But in reality, few of us are blessed with the ideal site. In this section, we'll also explore how to create beautiful borders in less-than-ideal settings—from damp shade and rocky soil to hot, muggy climates where many perennials wilt in summer.

SYDNEY EDDISON

teaches gardening at the New York Botanical Garden. The author of four gardening books, including *The Self-Taught Gardener,* she writes for several publications and lectures widely.

A Perennial
Border
for All
Seasons

Bulbs brighten the border with a splash of color in early spring. Designing a perennial border with periods of peak bloom provides season-long pleasure. Clumps of tulips and daffodils pepper the author's border in early May.

PLANTING A GARDEN of annuals is like discovering the fountain of youth—at least for a season. Their bright flowers remain relatively unchanged until they are snuffed out by frost. Perennials, on the other hand, are a constant, but ever-changing, presence. That is their great charm.

Each perennial blooms for a limited period, creating a dilemma for the gardener. How do you combine a variety of plants with different flowering times into a living collage that changes with the seasons? If you choose plants for a succession of bloom from spring through fall, you'll never have the big splashes that set your heart racing. But if you fill a border with plants that flower all at once, then color will be scarce before and after the crescendo. For those of us with perennial borders in full view of the house, one bold display per year simply is not enough.

In 32 years of designing and redesigning my large perennial border in southwestern Connecticut, I have come to

Plan for a succession of peaks. White tulips and purple-flowered grape hyacinths, still in their prime, will soon relinquish their place to a peony's bronze-red leaves.

accept the hard truth: you can't have it all. But you can have a great deal—as long as you don't insist on having it all at once. The answer is to compromise between having one great explosion of bloom or a long-running, but low-key, display. By choosing two or three distinct peaks of bloom and relying on a few annuals and some decorative foliage in between, you can have a garden that provides pleasure all year long.

FOCUS ON SEASONS OF PEAK BLOOM

Choosing the moments for high floral drama depends on your plant preferences, your lifestyle and, to some extent, the size of your flower bed. If you love a particular group of plants, then use them in your border as a peak. But whatever plants you choose to grow, get to know them well. Read about them and, if possible, observe them in other people's gardens.

Of course, there is no substitute for growing them yourself, but that takes time.

The pattern of your life can also guide you in choosing the moments for peak bloom in your garden. For instance, people who go to warm climates in the winter and come north only when summer is well on the way should consider growing summer-flowering perennials instead of daffodils and tulips, while gardeners who sail in the summer might want to stuff their gardens with spring bulbs and forget about daylilies.

The size of your border can dictate the number of peaks you can have. The more room you have from front to back, the more plants you can accommodate. In a shallow border, 4 ft. deep or less, you might have to limit yourself to bulbs for spring and one midsummer splash. But if you have a border twice as deep, you may be able to orchestrate three or four big displays.

My perennial garden has three high points: the early bulb display; the fleeting but lovely, period in late spring when the peonies, irises and rhododendrons bloom; and the flamboyant month of July when the daylilies strut their stuff.

BULBS ANNOUNCE THE ARRIVAL OF SPRING

You won't find spring-flowering bulbs in books on perennials, but they are a mainstay of the border at a time when few perennials flower. Because so many spring bulbs can be squeezed in among the perennials, having a colorful border in April and May is no great challenge. And since bulb foliage disappears by midsummer, even a small border can afford a lavish spring display. In my garden, white daffodils and white tulips light up the perennial border for at least five weeks beginning in

mid-April. While the short-lived tulips have to be replaced every few years, the daffodils are a permanent fixture.

Making the combination of perennials and bulbs work does require discipline, however. The foliage of spring-flowering bulbs must be allowed to ripen in its own good time in order to store food for next year's flowers. You may not, in good conscience, remove the yellowing foliage, nor can you constrict it by braiding or otherwise mangling it. You are left, therefore, with the problem of concealing it. Ideal for this purpose are the sweeping leaves of daylilies, clumps of *Sedum* 'Autumn Joy' and peonies.

Brilliant red peonies and lavender Siberian irises bring a second peak of bloom in late spring.

Perennials parade their summer color. The red and yellow trumpets of daylilies and true lilies, repeated throughout the border, herald the summer peak.

PERENNIALS CARRY LATE SPRING AND SUMMER

The second period of peak bloom in my garden was determined by plants discovered on the property when we moved here. A lavender-blue bearded iris growing by the front walk, along with some old-fashioned rose-red peonies, became the foundation of the May-June display. Several rhododendrons, which were among my first plant purchases, soon augmented this late spring high point. More by luck than by design, I planted them on the hillside behind the perennial border. They flower at the same time as the peonies and irises, and later on they provide an evergreen background for the other perennials.

Alas, adverse weather often curtails this period of bloom. Heavy rain is devastating to peonies, and an early heat wave can reduce trusses (clusters) of rhododendron flowers to dirty laundry. Nevertheless, given equable weather, this phase of pink, red, white, lavender and purple is lush and gorgeous.

Like most beginning gardeners, I started off with visions of a summer garden. I was teaching at a boarding school. The fall and spring terms were hectic, and the garden was a summer project. Therefore, my first perennials were midsummer bloomers: daylilies, globe thistles, coneflowers and sunflowers. They continue to put on a dazzling show from the middle of July into August.

"My late-season garden did not begin to take shape until I discovered blue-mist shrub."

USE SPECIAL PLANTS
TO EXTEND THE SEASON

I arrived at the late spring peony-iris-rhododendron period and the midsummer display quite early in my career, but I used to feel that the garden was over by the middle of August. Battles with Japanese beetles, high temperatures and humidity, and inadequate rainfall took their toll on both garden and gardener. By mid-August the only perennials in bloom were yellow daisies: sunflowers, rudbeckias and sneezeweed (*Helenium autumnale*).

My late-season garden did not begin to take shape until I discovered blue-mist shrub (*Caryopteris* × *clandonensis*), which blooms from mid-August to mid-September. With its gray-green foliage and tufts of fuzzy blue flowers, blue-mist shrub proved to be the cure for too much yellow. To my great pleasure and surprise, its long bloom season also overlapped with that of *Sedum* 'Autumn Joy', carrying the garden into September. *Sedum* 'Autumn Joy' is the perfect all-season perennial. It is beautiful from the moment the succulent blue-green leaves are visible in the spring until winter caps the dried flower heads with snow. In August, small, starry pink flowers open.

Ornamental grasses, mostly members of the genus *Miscanthus*, eventually displaced some of the sunflowers at the back of the border. Finally, a chance gift of a gorgeous purple aster (*Aster novae-angliae* 'Hella Lacy') put the finishing touch on the autumn garden. Although they don't quite add up to a peak, these late summer- and fall-flowering perennials help extend the season of bloom well past frost.

I am not a gardener who hates winter. In some ways, New England is at its bony best stripped of foliage. The essential character of the region is expressed in rocky ridges that stretch from Connecticut to Maine. In the gar-

den, the extreme contrast between the perennial border's stark winter appearance and its lush summer phase delights me. Particularly satisfying are the earthen hues of the grasses along with the pale, parchment skeletons of blue-mist shrub. In front of the grasses and the stiff dry stems of *Sedum* 'Autumn Joy', a fieldstone retaining wall that runs along the front of the border gives purpose and structure to my garden. It is the restraint of the winter landscape that prepares the gardener's palate for the abundance of spring and another year of bloom.

After a light snowfall in January, the flower heads of *Sedum* 'Autumn Joy' hold cotton balls of snow. Behind, the stalks of an ornamental grass rustle in the breeze, and the evergreen mounds of rhododendrons serve as harbingers of spring flowers.

How to Maintain Color between Peaks

Because her border is so crowded with perennials, the author has space only for annuals that take up very little room at ground level. *Verbena bonariensis,* with its clusters of tiny flowers borne at the ends of spare stems, fits the bill perfectly.

Between peaks of bloom, colorful foliage and contrasting leaf texture carry the show. The broad band of lamb's-ears, which holds the garden together all season, plays a dominant role when flowers are scarce.

It took several years of trying—always unsuccessfully—to have it all before I was able to accept the idea of the perennial garden as a checkerboard. If a square is occupied, it is occupied for the whole season. (Spring bulbs are the exception that proves the rule; they relinquish their squares to succeeding perennials by going dormant in the summer.) Despite the constraints of the checkerboard, I've found ways to help the garden look colorful between peaks. I rely on a few annuals for late summer color and a group of perennials that have reliably attractive foliage for the whole season. I also employ two design techniques to create the illusion of abundance, making a few flowers appear to be many.

THE VALUE OF A FEW ANNUALS

Although annuals are bit players in my garden cast, they are indispensible for their season-long bloom. They furnish dependable touches of color, while the perennials come and go around them. Cosmos is valuable for its small footprint (it has very little foliage at its base), thread-like leaves and its shallow, wide-open flowers in hues of white, pink and purple that weave and float among the perennials.

Verbena bonariensis, hardy in its home port of Buenos Aires, Argentina, but here treated as an annual, gets my vote for versatility. It takes up no room at its feet, branching low down with thin, rigid stalks. The terminal clusters of tiny mauve flowers add flecks of color without cluttering up the border with foliage. British gardening authority Christopher Lloyd referred to plants like verbena and cosmos as "see-through plants" because they can be used even in the front of the border without obscuring the view behind them.

THE IMPORTANCE OF FOLIAGE

The size, stature, structure and leaves of a perennial are as important as its flowers. Even the best and most persistently floriferous perennial has a period when it is not in bloom. Usually, this period far exceeds its flowering season, but you are stuck with the plant for the whole year, so it had better earn its keep.

To play its part adequately, foliage must retain its shape, color and carriage throughout the season. If the plant needs to be cut back after flowering, it must recover quickly. Foliage is especially critical in the case of edging plants. For plants in the middle of a well-stocked bed, a short period of vegetative ugliness is permissible. But plants at the front of the border don't have the luxury of taking a long break. Among my favorite perennials for the front of the border are the catmints (*Nepeta* spp.), with their mops of gray-green foliage and racemes of blue flowers; *Allium senescens* 'Glaucum', an ornamental onion that makes a swirling mat of gray-green leaves; and *Sedum* 'Ruby Glow', a hardy succulent that grows into a slightly sprawling, 10-in.-high mound of stems covered with red-edged, blue-green leaves.

Colorful foliage—silver, blue, purple and red—can be almost as effective as flowers in satisfying the eye as it craves color during pauses in the blooming season. The best thing I did for my border was to plant a broad band of gray-leaved lamb's-ears (*Stachys byzantina*) at the foot of the low retaining wall that runs the length of the garden. The lamb's-ears make one garden out of many plants, and by following the contours of the hillside, they anchor the bed to its site. For blue foliage, I have a clump of blue oat grass (*Helictotrichon sempervirens*), with its stiff but graceful gray-blue leaves. Purple leaves are a favorite of mine, including those of shrub smokebush (*Cotinus coggygria* 'Royal Purple'), perennial coral bells (*Heuchera micrantha* 'Palace Purple') or annual *Perilla frutescens*.

The most striking red-leaved plant in my garden is not a perennial but a weeping threadleaf Japanese maple (*Acer palmatum* var. *dissectum*) named 'Crimson Queen'. Even a young threadleaf Japanese maple is a thing of beauty; an old one that has been skillfully pruned is nothing short of spectacular. Mine is 20 years old and the most handsome plant in the border. The delicately cut, reddish foliage is as eye-catching as flowers all summer, and it's superb in the fall when it turns scarlet. In winter, the branches trace a zigzag pattern against the snow.

CREATING THE ILLUSION OF ABUNDANCE

With a little sleight of hand, you can give the impression that more is going on in your garden than actually is. One technique is to pair two well-matched plants that bloom simultaneously and repeat them throughout the border. They may be the only two plants in

flower, but plopped in tandem here and there in the garden, they create the illusion of abundance. Repetition, whether of color or form or both, also provides structure and order. In my garden, yellow, gold, orange and red daylilies are repeated throughout the summer border in association with spots of steel-blue from the globe thistles.

You can also make the most of a few flowers by siting your border so that it is viewed at an angle. Confronting a flower bed head-on exposes every gap. Viewing the bed obliquely conceals gaps; plants that may be some distance apart appear to be one behind another.

No matter what you do, a perennial border is never really finished. Plants such as peonies and daylilies are long-lived, and they eventually encroach on the space of less vigorous neighbors. So you edit here. You restrain there. You squeeze in one more plant somewhere else. That's what makes perennial gardening so fascinating.

(ABOVE) Bridging the gap. In early June, the far end of the author's border is awash in color.

(LEFT) A month later, with only a few daylilies and the yellow spires of a mullein in evidence, the red foliage of a cutleaf Japanese maple, the pincushion of blue oat grass leaves and the strip of gray lamb's-ears continue to enliven the scene.

INTA KROMBOLZ

is a member of the Hardy Plant Society and the Hosta Society. She makes and designs iron garden sculptures, and her garden in West Chester, Pennsylvania, is featured on tours yearly.

Solutions *for Wet,* Shady Sites

Once an overgrown thicket of brambles, vines, and weeds, this lush shade garden is now home to numerous plants that thrive in its damp, humus-rich soil.

A S OFTEN HAPPENS, inspiration comes when you least expect it. Driving to work one day, I spotted a man clearing underbrush on a wooded lot. I stopped and we talked, and before I knew it, I'd hired Russ Walters to clear a similar patch of woods for me.

The area Russ set to work on was a wooded area about 75 ft. long and 20 ft. wide at lower edge of our property. It was so overgrown with brambles, nettles, vines, skunk cabbage, and weedy shrubs that you could barely walk through it. And to make matters worse (or so I thought), the soil was perpetually moist. I'd used the area as a dumping ground for garden refuse, leaves, and broken branches. To disguise the mess, I planted a screen of butterburs (*Petasites japonicus*) and variegated grasses (*Miscanthus sinensis* 'Variegatus'). Both of these plants are vigorous growers and had spread with abandon through the area.

Texture and foliage are the star attractions in a shade garden. Ostrich fern (*Matteuccia struthiopteris*), *Rodgersia podophylla*, and *Carex siderosticha* 'Variegata' create a striking composition near the base of a tall tree.

> *"I did a lot of sloshing about with my umbrella to check where all the runoff areas were."*

~

If you have a similar "trouble" spot on your property, consider looking at the site with a fresh perspective. There are many beautiful plants that thrive in damp soil. If water naturally flows through your property, as it does in this area of mine, it's a wonderful opportunity—coveted by many a gardener who must settle for an artificial pond or water feature. Spreading beneath the cool canopy of mature trees, this shady, wet stretch of ground has become my most treasured garden area.

CLEAR THE SITE IN SECTIONS

Hiring Russ Walters was the impetus that got my project under way. I'd highly recommend getting some good, strong help to anyone tackling such an area. While Russ pulled out the shrubs, brambles, and vines, my husband, Skip, and my son, Steve, dug up the big clumps of grass and replanted them in various areas of the garden. I set to work digging out the butterbur and skunk cabbage.

What seemed like an insurmountable job slowly moved along because we took small areas, completely cleaned them out, and then moved on. While clearing can take place at any time of year, we did this work in winter because the weather was mild and the ground wasn't frozen. It sure beat sweating in hot, muggy July.

With all the scrub growth removed, we discovered a dry, rocky berm at the outer most edge of the area. A natural creek bed flowed along one side the berm, fed by underground springs and street runoff. This natural hollow followed a slight downhill course, meandered

around an elevated stand of mature oak, ash, and beech trees, and continued downward to empty into a creek that runs on the very edge of our property. It was an area of lovely natural beauty and wonderful potential.

I turned over all the soil to check its contents and also to aerate it. It looked like the perfect place to plant. Like most wooded areas, it contained a lot of natural compost from the many years of dumping and leaf fall. I noticed that in some places the soil was perfectly loamy and moist, but in other spots, below a layer of humus, the soil was like gray cheese—so dense, you could cut with a knife. If you're faced with heavy clay soil, work in as much organic matter as you can. It's likely that if the area is wooded, you'll have a good supply leaf mold and compost on hand.

PROVIDE DRAINAGE FOR RAIN AND RUNOFF

While I've come to learn that water can be a blessing, if left uncontrolled, it can also be a curse, washing away topsoil and plantings. We quickly had our first test—a week of heavy rain soon after the clearing was done. I did a lot of sloshing about with my umbrella to check where all the runoff areas were. The soil that had been turned over was so saturated it resembled the consistency of cooked oatmeal. I dug drainage channels that benefited the garden in two ways: they allowed the water to run off and they raised the soil level in the surrounding areas, helping it to drain more easily. The channels are about 1 ft. wide and deep. This was pretty much a trial-and-error

Combine plants that share a similar foliage color in different textures. Here, the bright chartreuse blades of grassy-leaved sweet flag grow in front of big, bold 'Sum and Substance' hosta, and purple shiso (*Perilla frutescens* 'Atropurpurea') provides a dark contrast.

procedure—just when I thought I had all the runoffs figured out, it would rain again and new ones would develop.

All of that water needed a place to go so I created a natural pond next to the berm. I dug out an area about 20 ft. long, 10 ft. wide, and 18 in. deep, tossing the soil on the edges for planting. The excavation unearthed rocks of various sizes that were used to line the edges of the pond. Then I built a spillway that would channel water overflow toward the stream. Drainage problems solved, the soil was ready for planting.

If you have a wet site without the benefit of a natural place for the water to go, like a stream, you'll have to create a solution. In this case, it would probably be wise to consult a

landscape professional about installing drainage and perhaps a dry well to handle water runoff.

CHOOSE PLANTS THAT THRIVE IN SOGGY SOIL

There is no greater delight to a true plant lover than a new garden with lots of room for planting. But before beginning any design, it's a good idea to look at the garden's existing structure and surroundings. The finest specimen in my damp, shady garden is a towering oak that stands in the group of trees next to the pond. In my mind, it became essential that any new plantings carry the eye to this majestic tree. Therefore, I designed the beds to be low in height, so as not to obscure the trees beyond. This also maintains the calm, wooded feeling of the area, as the tall trees still dominate the big picture, and the new understory plantings create a soothing carpet of foliage and texture.

"To keep the informal feel of the woods, I planted in large, natural drifts."

I was thrilled at the prospect of experimenting with plants in these damp, shady conditions. And, happily, I discovered many plants that are perfectly at home in moist soil. Many of them were transplanted from other gardens on our property with more normal soil conditions.

To keep the informal feel of the woods, I planted in large, natural drifts, usually grouping five or more specimens of one species together. In a shade garden, foliage and texture play starring roles in design, while flowers are a secondary consideration. In early spring, the bright magenta blossoms of Japanese primroses (*Primula japonica*) rim the pond and

stream-side, but the rest of the year the gardens are dominated by plants with bold leaves, like hostas, golden meadow sweet (*Filipendula ulmaria* 'Aurea'), and *Ligularia stenocephala* 'The Rocket'. The large foliage is offset by contrasting, feathery ferns and fine-leaved sedges.

I like to combine plants with similar foliage color that have contrasting leaf shapes and textures. For example, near a boulder path that weaves through the wettest area of the garden, I've planted golden, grassy-leaved sweet flag (*Acorus gramineus* 'Minimus Aureus'). Though this plant is only 3 in. tall, it stands out because of its bright chartreuse color. The same color is repeated nearby in the taller

An old potting shed anchors one end of the garden; its peeling paint suits the relaxed atmosphere of the woods. In front, beds are heavily mulched with wood chips to keep weeds down.

Acorus gramineus 'Oborozuki' and the magnificent leaves of 'Sum and Substance' hosta. A similar hue is picked up in the taller upright leaves of yellow flag iris (*Iris pseudacorus*).

There are a handful of bulbs that do well in damp garden conditions. In springtime, checkered lily (*Fritillaria meleagris*), quamash (*Camassia leichtlinii*), and summer snowflake (*Leucojum aestivum*) add a touch of understated elegance to tufts of emerging perennials. American turkscap lily (*Lilium superbum*) grows 6 ft. to 8 ft. tall in the damp, humusy soil and has redish-orange summer flowers. I also add some tropical interest with tender perennials that enjoy the wet earth like *Canna* 'Pretoria', *Colocasia* 'Black Magic', and *Colocasia esculenta* 'Illustris'.

CLEAN BEDS IN FALL AND THE POND IN SUMMER

By far, the most important maintenance work this garden requires is good fall cleanup. I've found that the combination of dampness and leaf cover can lead quickly to crown rot, fungus, and mildew problems because of a lack of air circulation. So every fall, we rake out fallen leaves and cut back all of the perennials except the grasses, which are left standing for winter interest.

After the garden is cleaned out, I spread a thick layer of mulch around the plants. We use wood chips that are delivered free of charge to us by local tree trimmers. It seems that the course texture of the chips is beneficial to the damp earth; as they get worked into the soil over the course of the season they help aerate the heavy clay. In spring, I broadcast a slow-release fertilizer on the beds, and also apply well-aged horse manure or compost selectively to plants that are heavy feeders.

The drainage channels also need to be dug out about once a year. They're wide enough to walk through with a narrow spade, and I dig as I go, tossing the sandy silt that's accumulated in them directly into the garden. Every few years I also clean the pond out of fallen leaves and silt, tossing the debris up onto the banks to enrich surrounding plantings. This task is most easily accomplished in late summer, as the pond tends to dry up by then.

I've gained immense pleasure and satisfaction in claiming this wet, wild, wonderful place. And that old saying is true: sometimes it's hard to see the forest for the trees. I didn't see the true potential and beauty of this space for years—though all along it was right under my nose. But then I met Russ Walters one fine day.

These Plants Like Moist Soil and Shade

BULBS

Camassia leichtlinii (quamash)

Fritillaria meleagris (checkered lily)

Leucojum aestivum (summer snowflake)

Lilium superbum (American turkscap lily)

GRASSES

Acorus gramineus 'Minimus Aureus', *A. gramineus* 'Variegatus', *A. gramineus* 'Oborozuki' (grassy-leaved sweet flag)

Carex elata 'Aurea' (Bowles' golden sedge)

Carex nigra (black-flowering sedge)

Carex siderosticha 'Variegata'

Hakonechloa macra 'Aureola' (Japanese forest grass)

Miscanthus sinensis 'Variegatus'

FERNS

Dryopteris wallichiana (Wallich's wood fern)

Dryopteris cycadina (shaggy sheild fern)

Matteuccia struthiopteris (ostrich fern)

Osmunda regalis (royal fern)

Polystichum acrostichoides (Christmas fern)

Selaginella braunii (spikemoss)

PERENNIALS

Artemisia lactiflora 'Guizhou' (white mugwort)

Aruncus dioicus 'Knieffii' (goatsbeard)

Astilbe × *arendsii* 'Fanal', *A. chinensis* var. *pumila*

Astrantia major (masterwort)

Caltha palustris (marsh marigold)

Corydalis lutea

Chelone lyonii (turtlehead)

Chrysogonum virginianum (green and gold)

Euphorbia dulcis 'Chameleon'

Filipendula ulmaria 'Aurea' (golden meadowsweet)

Hemerocallis cvs. (daylilies)

Hosta cvs.

Tricyrtis spp. and cvs. (toadlilies)

Iris ensata 'Variegata' (variegated Japanese iris)

Iris pseudacorus (yellow flag)

Iris sibirica (Siberian iris)

Ligularia stenocephala 'The Rocket'

Lobelia 'Ruby Slippers'

Rodgersia aesculifolia and *R. podophylla*

Petasites japonicus (butterbur)

Persicaria amplexicaulis and *P. bistorta* 'Superba' (fleece flower)

Primula japonica (Japanese primrose)

Sanguisorba canadensis (Canadian burnet)

Thalictrum rochebruneanum (meadow rue)

Veronicastrum virginicum (culver's root)

Viola labradorica (Labrador violet)

In early spring, bright pink Japanese primroses bloom in the damp soil near the hand-dug pond. Later in the season, interest in the garden comes from plants with beautiful foliage.

JIMMY & BECKY STEWART

have created their own style of southern cottage gardens using plants that will reliably perform in the Southeast. Their gardens have been featured on tours and in numerous publications.

Designing a
Warm-Climate
Border

Under reddening dogwoods, a southern garden blazes with fall color. Most of the flowers, including the yellow-orange *Zinnia haageana* and the scarlet firebush, are annuals, planted to play a starring role where summers are too hot for many perennials.

EACH SEASON, we're amazed at how broad our gardening opportunities are, despite the rigors of our climate. Rather than despair at the difficulties of gardening in the South, we have accepted the challenge. Wherever summers turn hot—the Southwest, the Plains, California and much of the Eastern U.S.—you can use our techniques.

As professional garden designers in Atlanta, Georgia, we're faced with fierce summers and mild winters, but we've discovered that we can re-create the look of traditional borders usually found in cooler climates. The crescendos of perennial flowers familiar to northern gardeners are impossible to duplicate in a climate where bloom time stretches over a much longer season and oppressive heat makes flowers come and go in a hurry. What's more, many perennials languish or even perish in the brutal heat and humidity of our summers. We grow just a core of perennials that we've found to be tried and true, and complement them with annuals and

Pinks, poppies, pansies and foxgloves in an Atlanta garden evoke the hues and textures of summer gardens in cooler climates. Because these plants cannot survive a long, hot growing season, the authors pull them up as summer approaches and replace them with heat-loving annuals.

perennials-grown-as-annuals to achieve and maintain a colorful display. You can too.

The rest of the year, we've also turned our climate to advantage. Our relatively mild winters allow us to have a second growing season. Many perennials that die back to the ground in colder climates remain evergreen here, and some cold-tolerant annuals can flower all winter long. In the fall, we also put in a variety of plants that love cool weather but abhor the heat. They flower magnificently in spring; then we pull them up and replace them with the annuals of summer.

YOUR PERENNIAL IS MY ANNUAL

We've had to forget most of what we learned from gardening books about "annuals" and "perennials." While some perennials are worthy of the name in the South, many old favorites, such as garden pinks (*Dianthus plumarius*) and Shasta daisies (*Leucanthemum* × *superbum*), invariably succumb to one or another of our environmental stresses. Plants are often rated by their cold-hardiness, but here we need heat ratings. Many cold-hardy plants are just no match for our combination of long, hot, humid summers and mild, wet

winters. In summer conditions, many plants overextend themselves, producing weak, floppy foliage that "melts," or rots, in the humidity. In winter, rain saturates the heavy clay soil that is common in many parts of the South. Most perennials, even many of those that tolerate wet feet while in active growth, rot if soil drainage is poor in the winter.

Since many plants on the traditional palette of perennials don't perform for us, we search out equally attractive new plants adapted to the South. For example, although most pinks, which perfume spring gardens in the North, can't stand up to our heat and humidity, we've found an ideal substitute in *Dianthus* 'Bath's Pink'. It has beautiful, mat-like, evergreen foliage and produces delightfully fragrant, single pink flowers for about four to six weeks in spring. We've also discovered a summer-tough Shasta daisy cultivar named 'Becky', sometimes sold as the July daisy. This selection yields numerous bright white daisies on stiff, erect stems from late June to August. Its rich green foliage is attractive year-round.

We also grow perennials that are not well known outside of the South because of their limited cold-hardiness (though, as is often the case, these plants are probably hardier than one might think). One of our favorites is the double Japanese aster, *Kalimeris mongolica*, which covers itself with small, white daisies from May to frost. We've also fallen in love with a sprawling, tropical-looking plant called *Tradescantia pallida* 'Purpurea'. We grow it for its long, purple, strap-like leaves, which combine wonderfully with silver-foliage plants. The unassuming pink flowers are an extra treat.

Not all of our reliable perennials are out of the ordinary. Some of the best perennials for the South are also popular in the North. The yarrow *Achillea* 'Coronation Gold', the purple coneflower *Echinacea purpurea* 'Bright Star' and the early blooming *Phlox maculata* 'Miss Lingard', for example, have all thrived consistently over many years.

SWAP PLANTS SEASONALLY

Keeping a garden looking its best year-round requires moving plants in and out with our two distinct seasons. We grow annuals to help extend color all year. Late fall through spring is our cool season. In October, we pull up heat-loving summer annuals and put in pansies (*Viola* × *wittrackiana*), poppies (*Papaver* spp.) and Johnny-jump-ups (*Viola tricolor*). They flower during winter warm spells and throughout the spring. In the fall we also plant perennials and biennials that thrive in cool, spring weather, but falter in our summer heat. The cool-season plants make their show in spring and then, as the weather warms up, usually in May, we dig them up and replace them with warm-season annuals and tender perennials to carry on the show until frost.

The technique of swapping out plants on a seasonal basis can be applied to gardens of all sizes, from large displays to small patio containers. And while it may sound like an expensive proposition, the enterprising gardener can easily reduce costs by starting annuals from seeds and by taking cuttings of tender perennials in the early fall and overwintering them indoors.

GARDENING IN THE COOL SEASON

By mid-October, we're ready to replace summer annuals with cool-season selections. Mid-October is our first frost date, but even if the weather stays warm, we don't wait for freezing temperatures to do our swapping; the cool-season annuals need time to become established if they're to put on their show in early spring. Pansies are the most popular cool-season annuals in our area because, barring extremely cold temperatures, they flower without interruption until the following summer. Other good cool-season annuals include Iceland poppies (*Papaver nudicaule*), China pinks (*Dianthus chinensis*) and Johnny-jump-ups. We buy plants in 4-in. pots for use in our clients' gardens, but you can also start seeds in late summer for fall transplanting.

Fall is also the best time to plant biennials, such as foxglove (*Digitalis purpurea*) and sweet William (*Dianthus barbatus*), and perennials, such as delphiniums (*Delphinium* spp.) and hollyhocks (*Alcea rosea*), that normally expire here due to the heat. These plants stay green all winter, then bloom reliably the following spring.

While some of our cool-season biennials and perennials might survive to bloom again next year, the chances are slim. So, as cool nights and mild days give way to mounting temperatures, usually around mid-May, we pull up the cool-season plants in preparation for our challenging summer.

❧

"Keeping a garden looking its best year-round requires moving plants in and out with our two distinct seasons."

How a Warm-Climate Border Changes with the Seasons

In a flower border for a warm climate, annuals and perennials-grown-as-annuals come and go in relays to complement a core of reliable perennials. In the sample border shown here, cool-weather annuals (green) provide color and foliage in winter and spring and give way to warm-season annuals (yellow) in the heat of summer, while a few perennials (blue) persist year-round.

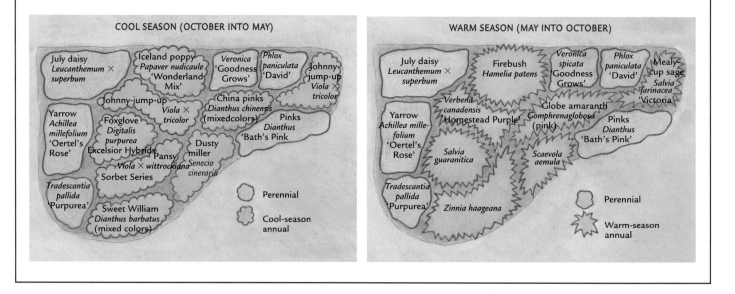

COOL SEASON (OCTOBER INTO MAY)

July daisy *Leucanthemum × superbum* — Iceland poppy *Papaver nudicaule* 'Wonderland Mix' — Veronica 'Goodness Grows' — Phlox *paniculata* 'David' — Johnny-jump-up *Viola × tricolor* — Yarrow *Achillea millefolium* 'Oertel's Rose' — Johnny-jump-up — Foxglove *Digitalis purpurea* Excelsior Hybrids — *Viola × tricolor* — China pinks *Dianthus chinensis* (mixed colors) — Pinks *Dianthus* 'Bath's Pink' — Dusty miller *Senecio cineraria* — Pansy *Viola × wittrockiana* Sorbet Series — *Tradescantia pallida* 'Purpurea' — Sweet William *Dianthus barbatus* (mixed colors)

Perennial
Cool-season annual

WARM SEASON (MAY INTO OCTOBER)

July daisy *Leucanthemum × superbum* — Firebush *Hamelia patens* — Veronica *spicata* 'Goodness Grows' — Phlox *paniculata* 'David' — Mealy-cup sage *Salvia farinacea* 'Victoria' — Yarrow *Achillea millefolium* 'Oertel's Rose' — *Verbena canadensis* 'Homestead Purple' — Globe amaranth *Gomphrena globosa* (pink) — Pinks *Dianthus* 'Bath's Pink' — *Salvia guaranitica* — *Scaevola aemula* — *Tradescantia pallida* 'Purpurea' — *Zinnia haageana*

Perennial
Warm-season annual

GARDENING IN THE WARM SEASON

During the summer, when even the best of our perennials tire out, we rely on a number of tough, long-blooming annuals. They offer a wide choice of heights and forms. Two of our best performers are globe amaranth (*Gomphrena globosa*), a 2-ft.- to 3-ft.-tall, branching plant with clover-like blooms available in many colors from deep purple to white, and *Zinnia haageana,* an 18-in.- to 24-in.-tall, spreading plant with vivid orange or white flowers. Both are available at our local garden centers. You can also start them from seeds.

For the hot months, we also grow some long-blooming, tender perennials. Many of the salvias and verbenas fit into this category. Excellent choices include *Salvia guaranitica*, a 4-ft.- to 5-ft.-tall specimen plant with royal blue flowers; the moss verbena (*Verbena tenuisecta*), a low, edging plant that opens its small, round, blue,

white or pink flowers all summer long; and star-cluster (*Pentas lanceolata*), a 3-ft.-tall, upright plant with star-shaped blooms, available in a range of colors from red to pink to lavender.

We've recently tried some new annuals. We especially like firebush (*Hamelia patens*). It forms a small, sprawling shrub that stands 3 ft. tall, with scarlet-orange, tubular flowers. We also recommend fairy fan flower (*Scaevola aemula* 'Blue Wonder'). It's a low ground cover with sky-blue, fan-like flowers. Both plants can be hard to find, but they're worth the search.

Once cooler nights and shorter days arrive, we are blessed with a final burst of color from the late-blooming perennials—notably fall anemones, asters, ornamental grasses and *Sedum* 'Autumn Joy'. They are even more spectacular combined with the still-vibrant summer annuals. When frost hits, it's time to start over again with a new look for winter and spring.

A Selection of Plants for a Sunny Southern Flower Border

NAME	FLOWERS	BLOOM TIME	HEIGHT X SPREAD	COMMENTS
Tried-and-True Perennials				
Achillea 'Coronation Gold'				
Achillea millefolium 'Oertel's Rose' (yarrow)	Rose, fades to white	May–frost	12 × 24	Good cut flower; pretty, fern-like foliage
Kalimeris mongolica (Japanese aster)	Small, white daisies	May–frost	24 × 24	Upright, mounding habit
Leucanthemum × superbum (daisy)	Large, white daisies	July	36 × 24	Excellent cut flower; evergreen foliage
Coreopsis verticillata 'Moonbeam' (threadleaf coreopsis)	Sulfur yellow	June–Oct.	24 × 24	Lacy foliage; dense, mounding habit
Dianthus 'Bath's Pink' (pinks)	Single, pink	April–May	6 × 24	Dense, blue-gray foliage; evergreen
Phlox paniculata 'David' (garden phlox)	White clusters	May–Sept.	36 × 24	Mildew resistant; deadhead for more blooms
Tradescantia pallida 'purpurea'	Lavender-pink	April–frost	12 × 12	Purple foliage; good for accent or contrast
Veronica spicata 'Goodness Grows' (speedwell)	Deep blue spikes	May–frost	12 × 12	Good cut flower; evergreen foliage
Warm-Season Annuals				
Hamelia patens (firebush)	Scarlet-orange	May–frost	36 × 36	Tender shrub with tubular flowers
Gomphrena globosa (globe amaranth)	Purple, pink, white	May–frost	36 × 24	Clover-like blooms; excellent dried flower
Pentas lanceolata (star-cluster)	Many colors	May–frost	36 × 24	Attracts hummingbirds and butterflies
Salvia farinacea (mealycup sage)	Blue or white spikes	May–frost	30 × 24	Good cut and dried flower
Salvia guaranitica	Royal blue	June–frost	48 × 36	Tender shrub; attracts hummingbirds
Scaevola aemula 'Blue Wonder' (fairy fan flower)	Blue, lobelia-like flowers	May–frost	6 × 36	Spreading ground cover
Verbena canadensis 'Homestead Purple' (vervain)	Pink, lavender, white	May–frost	9 × 24	Sprawling habit
Verbena tenuisecta (moss verbena)	Blue, pink, white	May–frost	6 × 24	Ground cover; finely textured foliage
Zinnia haageana (zinnia)	Yellow-orange, white	May–frost	8 × 24	Small daisies; sprawling habit
Cool-Season Annuals				
Dianthus barbatus (sweet William)	Deep pink-white	April–May	12 × 12	Excellent cut flower
Dianthus chinensis (China pinks)	White, pink, red	April–May	18 × 18	Single blooms on erect stems
Digitalis purpurea Excelsior Hybrids	Mauve, pink, white	May–June	48 × 24	Stately, spike-like blooms
Papaver nudicaule 'Wonderland Mix' (Iceland poppy)	Pink, yellow, orange	Feb.–May	24 × 6	Colorful, satiny blooms; great cut flower
Viola tricolor (Johnny-jump-ups)	Purple, blue, white	Nov.–May	3 × 3	Good as "filler" plant
Viola × wittrockiana (pansies)	Many colors	Nov.–May	6 × 6	Excellent bedding or border plant

KARIN OVERBECK

is a Master Gardener and volunteers at a nearby gardening center. Karin and her husband, Mike, live in a renovated one-room schoolhouse in Sturgeon Bay, Wisconsin.

Can't Dig Down?
Build Up

One-room school-houses were often built on untillable land, so the only way to garden is in raised beds. The Overbecks built these triangular beds from stone gathered on their property.

I N THE ERA of one-room schoolhouses, untillable land was either donated or sold to school districts. And that's exactly where my husband, Mike, and I set our roots 11 years ago—in an early-1900s, one-room, ivy-covered, brick schoolhouse in Sturgeon Bay, Wisconsin. We knew we had purchased a rocky site, but didn't realize the magnitude of the situation until we wanted running water. That's when we discovered that bedrock lay merely inches beneath the soil's surface on our property.

As one might imagine, this not only called for some serious earth-moving equipment to make way for water lines, but it also posed a challenge for the formal garden that I had planned to view from our 8-ft.-tall windows. Through sheer determination, I managed to plant several old roses my mother had given me by wedging them into crevices. But these roses had been in the family for more than 90 years, and as their new caretaker, I had serious doubts

"Now that the shrubs and perennials have filled out, we don't spend as much time or money on annuals."

Even small trees can be planted in raised beds. This weeping mulberry (*Morus alba* 'Pendula') is surrounded by lilies (*Lilum* spp.).

about their future in such dire conditions. So Mike, nice guy that he is, started work on a series of raised beds for my garden.

We decided on three triangular beds with stone walls for my formal garden. Two are 16 ft. by 20 ft. by 25 ft., while the center bed is 25 ft. by 25 ft. by 40 ft. Once we laid out the beds, Mike began gathering stones from our property. The base of the walls was created from stones measuring roughly 12 to 14 in. square with flat stones topping off the walls.

The corner stones anchoring the beds were a bit larger. Except for the back side of the center bed, which we raised to 3 ft. for aesthetic reasons, most of the beds are about 18 in. high. This height gives most plant roots plenty of room to grow. The grass paths between the beds are about 4 ft. wide, which allows us to maneuver the riding lawn mower and garden cart along a grassy strip.

Over the years, we've created many other raised beds throughout the yard, mostly using

materials at hand. In areas where the soil was not quite so shallow, we've merely mounded up piles of compost and mulch that taper to a path or border edged in 5-in. hardheads—round granite stones deposited from glaciers.

Mike also built 4-ft. by 8-ft. raised beds from 4x4 lumber for our vegetable garden. The beds are about 18 in. high, and I'm surrounding them with handmade blocks and bricks—poured concrete blocks inset with stained glass and colored tiles. I've also made round stepping stones to use throughout the garden.

CREATE YOUR OWN RICH SOIL

One of the advantages of raised beds is that you can create your own soil from scratch. Rather than purchase topsoil, we opted to fill our raised beds with compost. Not only would the compost be cheaper and easier to come by but it would also provide a richer soil for our plants.

In the formal garden, we added a layer of well-aged horse manure from the barn, then filled the rest with composted wood chips and leaf mulch. Keep in mind, unless you turn shredded leaf mulch regularly, it can take up to a year to break down before you can plant in it. Often, we'll cover the ground with a layer of newspapers before building a raised bed to kill grass and weeds and to speed the decomposition of this layer. If we are in more of a hurry to plant, we'll go ahead and dig out the sod.

One of the reasons our plants have done so well is that raised beds provide good drainage. In our case, the rich compost retains enough moisture to nourish the plants, while allowing excess water to drain away.

Morning glories (*Ipomoea* spp.) climb along the fence, which gives added dimension and textural interest to the raised stone beds.

I find that there are fewer weeds in my raised beds, as the walls are high enough to keep out lawn debris and weed seeds kicked up by the lawn mower. And as long as I keep the beds small, I never compact the soil by walking in them. In fact, I can sit along the edge of the beds and do my planting, weeding, or deadheading comfortably.

RAISED BEDS ARE MORE EXPOSED TO THE ELEMENTS

Perhaps the only real drawback to raised beds is that they are more exposed to the elements than beds that are dug in the ground. Raised beds will warm up more quickly in the spring, but they also get colder in the winter and are more exposed to winds.

I save the outer 18 in. of the beds for annuals and bulbs that need to be dug in the fall. Here the bulbs are easy to find in the loose soil. Perennials are best grown in the interior of the beds, where they are better protected from the fluctuating temperatures. Mike also built a rustic fence along the edges of the

"We've even planted some small trees in our raised beds, giving the beds a sense of formality."

Mounds of soil or compost can create raised beds where there is at least a little soil. Here, round granite stones keep the earth in bounds.

raised beds, so that I can grow annual vines like scarlet runner beans, morning glories, and sweet peas alongside the beds. I like the height this adds to my beds.

I cover my raised beds in early spring with straw or leaf mulch that is just beginning to compost. In addition to adding a fresh layer of organic matter, this mulch helps to retain

moisture and to keep weeds at bay. Since we get so much snow here, I don't mulch for the winter, but raised beds in warmer climates might benefit from some winter protection.

As long as plants are cold hardy, I've found that we can grow just about anything in our raised beds. They're the perfect home for my roses, lilies, and other perennials, as well as annuals, bulbs, and vines. We've even planted some small trees in our raised beds, giving the beds a sense of formality. So, if you think you have poor soil, don't despair. You can always garden in raised beds built from stone, lumber, bricks, concrete blocks, or even bales of hay—whatever materials you have at hand.

Chard, leeks, and basil thrive in this raised garden, surrounded by Karin's handmade stepping stones.

Compost makes a rich garden soil. Karin uses well-aged horse manure, wood chips, and leaf mulch, which she collects at little or no cost, to fill raised beds.

MARIE CASTELLANO

is a landscape designer and horticulturist. She is associated with the University of Illinois' Master Gardener program and teaches an evening class called "Gardening for Fun."

Sun *and* Shade

This garden was created to make the most of both sunny and shady spots. The curving beds pull it all together visually.

TO MOST GARDENERS, sun and shade conjure up images of separate gardens. But many gardens, including my own, have both sunny and shady areas. It can be a joy to have sun and shade, but when it comes to designing a cohesive landscape, it can also be a challenge.

In 1990, when I began work on my garden in Western Springs, Illinois (USDA Hardiness Zone 5), I found that there were areas of deep shade, dappled shade, and soft, filtered shade. In the middle of the yard was a bright, sunny swath, punctuated by two 30-ft.-tall spruce trees that cast long shadows—all this in a yard just 90 ft. wide.

To unify all of these diverse areas, I employed a series of simple design techniques that draw both your eyes and your feet through the garden, oblivious to sun or shade. By repeating shapes, colors, plants, materials, and focal points, the garden gained an overall sense of cohesiveness.

CREATE A FRAMEWORK FOR YOUR GARDEN

I began creating my garden much like an artist would a painting. The soil was my canvas, to which I added a frame of flagstone edging. Two layers of 4-in. flagstone surround my curving palette-shaped perennial gardens, creating a series of raised beds. The first layer is half-buried for stability; the second gives it some height.

Hardscaping materials are also the bones of my landscape, giving it dimension and character any time of year. So the flagstone that frames my raised beds also flanks my garden

"A pathway is a lot like a red carpet; it controls the way a garden is viewed."

paths and is used to create patios between the perennial borders. Overall, the effect is that of a single garden edged in stone—even though it encompasses sunny and shady areas.

A descending layer of trees and shrubs provides a pleasing background for the perennials in my sunny garden, just as they might in a painting. The 30-ft. spruces anchor each of the beds, while shrubby, purple-leaved plums (*Prunus cerasifera* 'Newport') fill in between them. A shorter hedge of northern bayberry (*Myrica pensylvanica*) was placed in front of the plums. In the foreground are flowering perennials—the subject of my garden painting.

A similar layer of trees, shrubs, and perennials was planted in the shade garden for balance and consistency. The plants are different, but the effect is the same. Even in winter, when the perennials have died back, these gardens are linked visually. The trees and shrubs—both deciduous and evergreen—help me survive the dreary winters by offering beautiful, snow-covered displays.

USE PATHWAYS AS A GUIDE

A pathway is a lot like a red carpet; it controls the way a garden is viewed. Straight paths direct your attention to a final destination,

Diverse garden areas are linked visually by flagstone edging and a subtle color scheme. Accent plants, like Japanese maple, are also repeated throughout the garden.

Between the flagstone edging, I covered my shaded paths with several inches of oak mulch. This same mulch is used throughout the yard as a ground cover for many plantings, providing yet another visual link.

REPEAT COLORS IN FLOWERS AND FOLIAGE

As a designer, I wanted my garden to be both a teaching and test garden, so it contains many different plants. For them to look as though they belonged together, I used a unified color scheme. I chose a palette of mostly pastel hues—a gradation of bright and pale tones of pink, lavender, and purple, with soft, subdued shades of blue and yellow. Purple coneflowers (*Echinacea purpurea*), silvery blue lamb's ears (*Stachys byzantina*), pink snapdragons (*Antirrhinum majus*), and yellow coreopsis (*Coreopsis verticillata*) are just a few of the annuals and perennials that fill my sunny borders.

However, to use the colors effectively, they had to be repeated in the shade garden. Here, witch hazel (*Hamamelis virginiana*) and lady's mantle (*Alchemilla mollis*) add a touch of yellow, while old-fashioned bleeding hearts (*Dicentra spectabilis*) display delicate, drooping, pink blossoms. Astilbe (*Astilbe* × *arendsii*) offers plumes of pink, white, and rose, and Bethlehem sage (*Pulmonaria saccharata* 'Mrs. Moon') displays bluish-pink blossoms. But since most shade-loving perennials bloom for only a short time, I rely primarily on foliage for excitement and color in the shade garden. My astilbe is also valued for its often rose-colored foliage and, after blooming, the spotted leaves of Bethlehem sage enliven the garden until the first frost. I also appreciate epimediums and caladiums for their colored foliage.

A single plant used in repetition provides another visual connection. One of my favorites is the Japanese maple (*Acer palmatum*). I have

Focal points draw the eye from one part of the garden to another. Whether an arbor (ABOVE), a carefully placed statuary (OPPOSITE LEFT), or a fieldstone patio (OPPOSITE RIGHT), these accessories pull a garden together and give it character.

while meandering paths add a sense of suspense to a garden. You never know what lies around each bend. That's why I like to include a winding path whenever I'm working on a wooded shade garden. In my own garden, a path divides the shade into three distinct areas, each with differing light conditions. This makes it easier to select and grow plants. The path also makes the shade garden look larger, as though an empty room were filled with furniture.

different cultivars in sun and shade, but the deep, reddish purple leaves and lacy foliage are echoed throughout the garden. On each side of the shaded garden path is a curved boxwood hedge. On a larger scale, 15 boxwoods (*Buxus microphylla* var. *koreana*) surround a display of daylilies in a sunnier section of the garden. And finally, another boxwood hedge delineates the end of the shade garden, where the lawn begins.

ADD FOCAL POINTS—
THE PERFECT ACCESSORY

Years ago, in my first landscape design class, my teacher taught me the importance of using focal points in a garden. Whether they are special plantings, hardscaped areas, or smaller structures, these focal points work almost as a magnetic force, drawing your attention to carefully chosen areas in the landscape.

I opted to use focal points in two ways. First, I created patios and provided places to sit for a while in the transitional areas of the garden. I also placed statuary throughout the garden to draw your eye from one point to another. Small stone cherubs, bunnies, and birdbaths are strategically sited to guide you step by step through the garden. And the sound of a water fountain in the shade garden tempts you to continue wandering along the winding path in search of its location. Sometimes it's these little accessories that really pull a garden together.

Having both sun and shade in a single garden may present a design challenge, but I have found this combination of contrasting light conditions offers advantages as well. When the heat of a summer afternoon makes working in the sun unbearable, the shade garden is waiting for me only steps away—cool and refreshing.

Credits

PHOTOS

Front matter

Delilah Smittle, © The Taunton Press, Inc.—p. ii

Gary Irving—p. iii

Steve Silk, © The Taunton Press, Inc.; Allan Mandell; Allan Mandell; Lee Anne White, © The Taunton Press, Inc. (top); Gary Irving (bottom)—Contents (from left)

Allan Mandell—p. 2

Part I: Design Strategies

Susan Kahn—pp. 4, 6, 8, 9, 10, 12, 28, 31, 36

Steve Silk, © The Taunton Press, Inc.—pp. 5, 14, 17, 18

Lee Anne White, © The Taunton Press, Inc.—pp. 20, 23, 25 (bottom)

© Allan Mandell—pp. 22, 25 (top), 27

Renee Beaulieu—pp. 30, 35

© Paddy Wales—p. 32 (Elizabeth England garden)

Chris Curless, © The Taunton Press, Inc.—p. 34

Part II: Great Border Plants

Lee Anne White, © The Taunton Press, Inc.—pp. 40, 42, 43, 44, 45, 46, 47, 62–63 (bottom), 68 (right)

© Clive Nichols—pp. 48 (The Priory, Kemerton, Worcestershire), 51, 53 (bottom), 54 (courtesy Meadow Plants, Berkshire), 55

© Bard Wrigley—p. 49

© Ken Druse—p. 50

© J. Paul Moore—p. 52

© Erica Glasener—p. 53 (top)

Steve Silk, © The Taunton Press, Inc.—pp. 56, 57, 58, 59, 60

© Jerry Howard—pp. 62 (top left), 68 (left)

© John Glover—pp. 39, 62 (bottom left), 64 (bottom), 65, 69

© Joseph G. Strauch, Jr.—pp. 62–63 (top), 64 (top)

© Pam Spaulding—p. 66

Chris Curless, © The Taunton Press, Inc.—pp. 70, 73 (right), 74

© David Cavagnaro—p. 72

© Peter Lindtner—p. 73 (left)

© Allan Mandell—pp. 76, 83, 88, 92

Linda Wesley, © The Taunton Press, Inc.—pp. 38, 80, 82, 84, 85

Delilah Smittle, © The Taunton Press, Inc.—pp. 86, 90 (center and bottom)

Mark Kane—p. 89

© Jane Grushow—pp. 90 (top), 93

© Charles Mann—p. 91

Part III: Special Techniques

© Allan Mandell—pp. 94, 96, 98, 99, 101, 106 (Linda Cochran garden, Bainbridge Island, Wash.), 107 (Sandy Argue garden, Victoria, B.C., Canada, designed by Eryl Morton), 116, 118, 119, 122, 123

© J. Paul Moore—pp. 95, 102

© Ken Druse—p. 104

Lee Anne White, © The Taunton Press, Inc.—pp. 105, 108, 110

© Tracy DiSabato-Aust—pp. 114, 115

Steve Silk, © The Taunton Press, Inc.—p. 121

Chris Curless, © The Taunton Press, Inc.—pp. 124, 126–131

Part IV: Garden Gallery

Mark Kane—p. 134

Chris Curless, © The Taunton Press, Inc.—pp. 132, 136–141

Linda Wesley, © The Taunton Press, Inc.—p. 148

© Becky Stewart—pp. 150, 152

Lee Anne White, © The Taunton Press, Inc.—pp. 133, 142, 144, 146, 147, 149, 156, 158–161

© Gary Irving—pp. 162, 164–167

ILLUSTRATIONS

Rosalind Loeb Wanke, © The Taunton Press, Inc.—p. 11

Lee Anne White, © The Taunton Press, Inc.—p. 24

© Christine Erikson —pp. 111–113